Praise For Howard R. Freedman And This Book

"My oldest child is a college junior and I've had the pleasure of Howard's advice and assistance since my son's senior year in high school. Howard got me through all of my issues so smoothly, and made the college financing process completely painless. Just as importantly, his calm demeanor helped lessen my anxiety through it all! Read the book and call the man, you will be fortunate to have his help!"

-Steven J Morton, Attorney,
SJM and Associates, Chicago, Illinois

"Howard Freedman has done an outstanding job helping to make college financing possible for my three daughters, even when obstacles made college financing look impossible. I recommend him as one of the foremost experts in his field along with his book that exemplifies his wealth of knowledge and dedication to his profession."

Jack B Garvey, Webmaster,
Little Rock School District, Little Rock, Arkansas

"Howard's affable demeanor as ACCESS Program Manager and Advisor at our school while working with students and parents from various backgrounds often confused by the financial aid process enhanced his effectiveness on what they needed to accomplish. Making College Happen: The Realities of Coping With College Costs *is a great testimonial to Howard's wealth of knowledge and commitment to providing the financial solutions to make college possible."*

-Maureen O'Donnell, Guidance Counselor,
Boston Community Leadership Academy,
Boston Public Schools, Boston, MA

"In all my years of collaboration with organizational representatives, I have never associated with a more professionally competent, concerned, dedicated, ethically responsible and personally congenial individual than Howard Freedman. His wise consultation and agreeable interpersonal style was vital in averting conflict among students and institutions."

-William Quill; Professor of Counseling Psychology, Coordinator of the School Counseling Program, Northeastern University, Boston, MA.

"As a retired Boston Police Officer, I worried that college for my son would be very expensive and leave him with many student loans after graduation. Howard seized every opportunity to save us money and coached us through the complexities of applying for and maximizing our financial aid package. We are forever grateful for all of his help."

-Audrey Fleming, Canton, MA.

*"*Making College Happen—The Realities of Coping With College Costs *is a well-written and honest resource on target for helping families to make informative college and financial decisions."*

-Professor Eric Freedman, Michigan State University, Pulitzer Prize-Winning Journalist and Author of *How to Transfer to the College of Your Choice*

"We appreciated Howard's expertise and communicative style when assisting us with completion of our daughter's FAFSA and CSS Profile. He provided excellent service in a non-judgmental manner and we would not hesitate to recommend Howard to other families who would benefit from someone who knows the ins and the outs of financial aid forms."

-Mary Brown-Jones, Guidance Counselor, Randolph, Massachusetts

MAKING COLLEGE HAPPEN

The Realities Of Coping With College Costs

by Howard R. Freedman

Founder, Financial Aid Consulting

Contents

CHAPTER 1

What's The Deal With Making College Happen?

"Education's purpose is to replace an empty mind with an open one."

- Malcolm Forbes

Skyrocketing college costs have become serious challenges to families who must cope with one of the most important decisions that they are likely to make. While college affordability and student debt are being addressed and publically debated within both academic and political communities, significant changes will not occur overnight. Consequently, families must be diligent in gathering accurate information in their pursuit of finding educational institutions that provide the best academic fit at the most affordable prices.[1] Fortunately, there are a wealth of options and solutions that exist to meet each family's unique financial circumstances.

College is only one of many types of higher education available to those who wish to continue beyond high school. Because of its high sticker price, it is not unreasonable to question whether a college education is worth it, especially in terms of its return on investment from the ensuing career path to which it may lead. This holds especially true for those students who feel pressured and

---

1 See my article on this: http://diverseeducation.com/article/16241/

uncomfortable with committing to a college or major. It's also true for those students who do not have the grades or credentials for acceptance into a quality college program and have not thoroughly evaluated if potential employers upon graduation will value the cost and type of degree.

Families, however, should not despair and remain open-minded about other, more affordable options that may lead to better results. They should also realize that a student should not attend college because they are forced to or are concerned about how they may be perceived by others. They should attend college if they are goal oriented and will work diligently to reach one. If not, community colleges, on-line learning, vocational schools, the military, and part-time programs are all viable alternatives that may provide better higher educational values.

Regardless of the choice, financial aid to pay for higher ed-ucation is only one element of a much larger process that many families may not fully comprehend. It is a resource that should be pursued even though it seldom covers all of the costs of college. As a result, families must be well positioned to leverage their liquid assets in conjunction with prudent borrowing and effective schol-arship search strategies.

This book seeks to inform parents of college bound students of the variety of options that they can utilize to better educate themselves on the many complexities that encompass the college decision making process. It also serves as a guide to the resources that are available for the most appropriate advice for their financial and familial situations. As a financial aid consultant, I have in-cluded many personal anecdotes, techniques, and strategies to cope with the financial and emotional costs of affording college with my hope that this book will lead families down the right path towards making college happen.

In 2002, when I created Financial Aid Consulting,[2] my mis-sion was to help families complete the FAFSA,[3] a form required by

2 www.financialaidconsulting.com

3 Access FAFSA here: https://fafsa.ed.gov/FAFSA/app/fafsa

colleges for federal and some institutional financial aid. It didn't take long to discover that parents were stressed and overwhelmed about completing this form rather than about how it worked in the overall financial aid process. Many were confused by what they were told by other parents, frightened by what they heard at financial aid presentations, and unsure about what to do next. Sadly, I witnessed parents fraught with despair agonizing over these challenges when I realized that they needed help beyond just completing financial aid forms. It was clear that the best way to deliver value-added services was to stop their suffering, anguish, and emotional angst by dealing with the facts and offering the best-educational alternatives and financial solutions available to satisfy their needs.

Completing financial aid forms is just the beginning of a much longer process. Parents often breathe a sigh of relief when they complete these forms without realizing that the work and decision-making process are far from over. The results from the FAFSA that calculate a family's EFC (Expected Family Contribution) are only estimates that do not always provide an accurate determination of how much a family can truly afford to pay for college since the FAFSA is based on averages and makes many assumptions without regard to the exceptions to the norm. Variables such as consumer debt, cash flow, credit worthiness, and special circumstances are only a few of the many elements that aren't factored into any financial need calculations and are sadly, often overlooked when financial aid is awarded. Consequently, financial aid and affordability can be significantly compromised when a family is unaware of how to identify and articulate this information to college financial aid officers. This also holds true for some private and public colleges that also use another form-the CSS/Financial Aid Profile[4] for institutional aid that comes from the college's coffers rather than from federal funds. Although it is more extensive than the FAFSA and provides explanatory sections, it still may not calculate an accurate estimate of how much a family can actually contribute to the cost of college.

---

4 http://student.collegeboard.org/css-financial-aid-profile

Coping with college costs is similar to coping with the high costs of owning a home, car, or other major purchase in that college is a costly investment that should be fully evaluated before deciding whether or not it will satisfy a family's needs. It takes defining criteria, thorough research and analysis, multiple campus visits and meetings, and knowing the net cost and financing options before making a final commitment. Finding the best college to fit a family's criteria should never be decided based on emotion, guilt, pressure, or rolling the dice and taking a chance on lady luck. It is a serious and expensive process that cannot be decided upon unilaterally by threat, coercion, peer pressure or based on money alone. It needs to be a partnership between the parent(s) and the student. A partnership in which well-defined educational goals and fit are evaluated and coupled with the financial resources to justify the true benefit and value of that education over the long haul. As long as both parties know the parameters and responsibilities and can plan ahead it will be a much more pleasant journey for creating the next chapter in life's journey beyond high school.

It is for these reasons that it is worthwhile to seek the services of a reputable and well-established financial aid consultant that can help families provide the proper direction to enable students to further their education. These services can help each family to focus on the big picture, identify any red flags, analyze each financial aid award, and then decide if it makes sense to accept or appeal it. Obtaining the right advice before making impulsive decisions or relying on opinions alone may be the best way to avoid the serious bottlenecks that may prevent a student from attending the best and most affordable college.

CHAPTER 2

How Do You Deal
With Uncertainty?

"Men build too many walls and not enough bridges."

- Isaac Newton

The journey to college is an assumed stressor for which most families expect to encounter conflict, sleepless nights, and guilt. Although some are well prepared to meet this challenge, others fall victim to negativity, despair, and self-doubt that can often impede effective planning and decision-making. Consequently, managing emotions and attitudes during these challenging times will play a key role in coping with college costs.

How do you deal with uncertainty?

One analogy to describe how emotions can impact thinking likens the college decision-making process to visiting an amusement park attraction:

Imagine a pitchman outside a popular attraction called "Journey of The Unknown" barking about the mysticisms inside. Clara, an aspiring college student, who is walking past at the time, is enticed to buy a ticket to the "most amazing experience of a lifetime." She knows nothing about it but decides to take the risk anyway. After paying admission, she enters a dark tunnel where creepy characters pop up from behind dark corners to surprise and scare her. Clara's emotions run the gambit from fright and laughter to despair as she questions why she made such an impulsive decision. On the other hand, her rational side recognizes that it is only a short journey and that there will be a light at the end of the tunnel. When it is over, she feels a little shaken but also a sense of relief knowing that she is safe and more confident about what to expect if she were to make a return visit.

Similarly, the road to college can also be laden with surprises and scary moments, yet it will be a much more comforting and pleasant journey by getting all the facts and setting realistic goals.

What Are The New Meanings Of YES And NO?

To help parents explore the emotional challenges that families are likely to encounter during the financial aid process, I've decided to create two clever acronyms for the words YES and NO.

I've defined "YES" as Your Emotional State. As most people are not eternal optimists, their emotional states must be fine-tuned throughout the financial aid process. Through no personal fault, emotional states may be affected by horror stories from their friends and families, information overload, and high school financial aid presentations. These can lead parents to believe that they are not qualified for financial aid, while feeling the doom and gloom from the media about rising college costs and escalating student debt.

The "NO" acronym is an oxymoron, or contradicting statement, that I've defined as Negative Optimism. These are the mixed emotions that parents feel when the pride and joy of raising a recent high school graduate are countered by the remorse and guilt of not having enough to pay for college. It is when parents are emotionally conflicted as they look forward to the future while reflecting on the past and what they should have done to become better prepared to pay for college. It would be similar to the feelings one might have when a despised in-law drives your uninsured new BMW off a cliff.

These YES and NO acronyms are meant to serve as reminders that there is positive hope for the future and no need to feel any Negative Optimism as problems or opportunities do offer solutions. You just need some help to understand where those solutions are.

How About Being Honest About How You Feel?

People often use and often misuse the words YES and NO in terms of their common meanings. Sometimes spontaneous answers to simple questions can lead to trouble if more information is needed. That is why it makes little sense to be pressured into making quick yes or no decisions without consideration of their ramifications.

Let's look at the typical conversations that occur between parents and their college-bound students when discussing college:

What Are The Closed-Ended Questions?

- Will you pay for my college education?
- Will you co-sign all of my student loans?
- Will you pay more for a state college if I go there?

These are examples of closed-ended questions from your children that can't, and shouldn't be answered easily with a simple yes or no without further thought and discussion.

Let's now analyze the pitfalls of closed-ended answers to each of my examples:

- Will you pay for my college education?

The word 'all' means everything, and including the out of pocket and borrowing options that can be a staggering amount of money. Before answering, parents should know each college's cost of attendance and average financial aid package by using each college's Net Price Calculator to quantify the estimated projected net annual costs after financial aid. Without such data, answering yes is no different than signing a blank check.

- Will you co-sign my student loans?

Most non-governmental (alternative) student loans require credit worthy co-signors. This is because students, in general, do not have established credit histories and are higher credit risks. Parents or other qualified co-signors must understand the potential, but very real, risk of being stuck with the bill, especially if the student does not make timely repayments. They should also analyze the value of a college education and if it is worthy of a high debt load before answering yes.

- Will you pay more for a state college if I go there?

The net price of in-state tuition at some state schools is not necessarily less than a private college. This is why it is so important to compare colleges in terms of the financial aid awards and quality of the education before paying for in-state or more costly state colleges for non-residents in other states.

Should Parents Be Obligated To Pay For A College Education?

Students wishing to continue their education beyond high school should be commended for taking advantage of the life opportunities that higher education affords. On the other hand, they should also realize that it is neither an entitlement nor does there exist a contractual agreement that requires parents to drain their financial assets or test their emotional endurance and stamina to allow them to do so. It is a serious journey in which parents must be discreet and honest with their yes or no answers. It is also a time to address ownership, accountability and empowerment issues to ensure that the student's and parent responsibilities are addressed before, and not after college acceptance.

How Do You Improve Communications?

Because of the cell phone and Internet technologies, people are communicating more than ever. Technology has offered the tools to report emergencies, the ability to communicate with clients, and limitless sources of information. However, has it enabled people to take the time to be effective listeners and communicators? Whatever, the circumstances, effective communication is not about technology, but committing the time to discuss and listen, not just hear one another, especially when dealing with the realities of the college decision-making process.

At times, it may seem that students and parents speak different languages or come from other planets entirely. This is because the mental wiring, priorities and life experiences are much different between the two groups. Adults are the pragmatists that have endured and overcame the real world social and economic challenges compared to the more idealistic hopes and dreams of their college bound students. Their goal is to do what is best even though both may chose to travel down different paths. Because of this, bridging the communications gap between both sides should not be a "winner takes all" competition, but rather a well-thought game plan that ensures that both the student and their parents are on the same track.

Communications can be simplified by following these few simple rules:

- Let the student research which colleges meet their educational and professional objectives.

- Discuss the criteria for choosing each college.

- Always have an affordable safety school.

- Plan campus visits.

- Discuss how much can be contributed as a parent to the student's education regardless of which school they would attend.

- Clarify how much loan debt the student can expect to incur including accrued interest to be paid after they graduate.

- Explain the extent of a parent's responsibilities if there is a need for a cosignor for the student's loans and the student's responsibility for making timely payments.

- Compose and approve a student / parent contract stating what grades the student is expected to maintain, accountability, financial responsibilities, and consequences.

- Empower the student to make the ultimate decision once they agree to the terms and conditions of your contract.

Humor Is A Great Stress Reliever

"Through humor, you can soften some of the worst blows that life delivers. And once you find laughter, no matter how painful your situation might be, you can survive it."

~Bill Cosby

Another important coping tool is using humor to deal with stress, especially during the pre-college years. Humor is an effective way of easing the pain and stresses of communicating with a college bound teenager especially when tough decisions must be made. Humor is not intended to make light of these serious and often emotional exchanges but rather a powerful way of taking the edge off of the intense stressors that families are likely to encounter.

This journey is not meant to be a scary ride. By making fun of ourselves and seeking the humor in even the most nerve-wracking situations, we can turn stress into positive energy and more effectively deal with the pains of affording college. After all, it is only a short voyage with a few bumps on the road. When it is over, there will be plenty of laughter at all of the adventures and misadventures, and all of the problems, also known as "opportunities," that were resolved.

What Are The Bad Reasons To Attend College?

I am often amazed at why some students have put so little effort into narrowing a college list. This is often the first costly mistake that can drive parents into directing hard earned money and loan commitments in the wrong direction. Below are some of the most unacceptable reasons for a student's college choice that parents should not be committed to support:

- My friend is going there.
- I got something in the mail that will guarantee a scholarship.
- They have a great golf team.
- It is in a warmer climate.

- My guidance counselor said that it's the only school that would accept me.
- They have a lot of weekend activities.
- I love their fitness center.
- I want to live as far away from home as possible.
- I love their TV commercials.

These reasons don't address cost, value, majors, quality of education, debt, or what that degree would be worth upon graduation. It is for these reasons that I stress the value of effective planning in order to overcome emotional and irrational choices throughout a student's decision-making college process. To provide structure to overcome the fears of this harrowing process and, hopefully, make this journey more pleasant, I've created an acronym for the word COLLEGES: Communications, Organization, Logistics, Limitations, Eligibility, Goal Setting, Evaluation, and Support.

How Should The Student Plan To Get To COLLEGES?

- **C**ommunications - A must for effectively ensuring that both parents and students understand what needs to be done in terms of identifying colleges, costs, and responsibilities. This shouldn't be based on wishful thinking but on honest, upfront dialogue. This is especially important when a student is focused on college admissions without regard to whether their parent(s) can afford it.

- **O**rganization - Purchase a notebook, storage files, or utilize an on-line system to keep everything easily accessible. Simplify the process by sorting everything in logical sequences that makes the most sense. Donate or recycle unnecessary documentation to ensure the focus is on the student's top 10 schools. Spreadsheets are also an excellent way to keep things well organized.

- **L**ogistics - Plan campus visits at convenient times and within proximity to each other. A well-planned campus visit is a critical step for evaluating both the feel and the fit of the student's needs.

- **Limitations** - Discuss the financial and logistical criteria for college selection. Include the costs for each application, financial contributions, and use each college's Net Price Calculator to estimate net costs. This is where communication and answering yes and no questions honestly will clarify the overall parameters for college selection and potential debt.

- **Eligibility** - How high does the student want to aim? Can they get in? Do they want to be a top student at a top school where everyone is a top student or truly be a top student at a quality institution, which is less competitive? Be realistic by considering admission criteria, acceptance rates and whether it is worth taking test preparation courses for increasing SAT or ACT test scores for colleges that are a stretch or are too competitive to realistically succeed.

- **Goal Setting** - Students need to articulate why they want to go to college, the degree they wish to pursue, and what that degree will be worth after graduation. It should not be related to what others are doing, or be justified if the major or school does not result in a rewarding position after graduation.

- **Evaluation** - There are other options to college that may provide better long-term value or opportunities. Don't just rely on the list that guidance counselors provided or colleges that are geographically popular. Consider Canadian and other foreign colleges that may provide great educations at much lower prices. Gap years, community college, the military, on-line programs, and trade schools are all worthy of consideration. It is important that students should know that their parents' love for them would not be conditioned on attending college but on finding the best opportunities.

- **S**upport - Recognize that high school guidance counselors and free resources can provide limited support for this process. Other services are economically priced[5] and can provide financially related services to clients throughout America. More extensive college preparation and testing services are also available depending on the family's budget. Always check the quality of the services, price, and avoid signing any costly contracts.

---

5 www.financialaidconsulting.com

CHAPTER 3

Who Can Help Me?

"Individual commitment to a group effort - that is what makes teamwork, a company work, a society work, a civilization work."

-Vince Lombardi

The good news about making college happen and the realities of coping with college costs is that no one is alone. In addition to the services of a reputable financial aid consultant, families can expect to interact with a wide array of resources that will provide varying degrees of support on the road to college. Here are some resources that will likely be encountered:

1. Friends, Family And What You Overheard

Many pieces of information about paying for college from those that have experienced it are worth pursuing. Feedback is healthy and encouraged so long as parents keep an open mind and realize that each student's credentials and family's financial circumstances are different. Network with others to find out as much possible from those whose advice is personally valued. Separate fact from opinion while recognizing that this is a decision-making process involving multiple resources to help a family discover which college offers the best opportunities and is most affordable for their student.

2. Financial And Legal Expertise

Financial aid consultants can also work with other resources, especially when it involves financial planning, tax filing, and even legal matters involving custodial and non-custodial parents. These relationships are important because each situation has an impact on financial aid eligibility within a much larger picture. More specifically, here are a few examples of where the following services impact financial aid:

- Tax Planning: The timing and reporting of income, capital gains, tax filing status, interest, dividends, business, personal and untaxed incomes, rental income, etc. will impact expected family contributions. Some may also be exceptions requiring further explanation.

- Financial Planning: College financing is part of a much broader spectrum of "birth to death" financial strategies. These include 529 college savings plans, tax-sheltered investments, cash flow, retirement income, sources and uses of funds, or simply answering questions about accessing assets to pay for college.

- Family Law: Issues and opportunities that may arise regarding how alimony, child support, and college contributions will impact financial aid and college affordability. These topics should be discussed before, and decided after the consummation of final divorce agreements.

Tax Professionals are responsible for personal, business and estate tax filing management and consulting. Although some may offer to fill in the FAFSA, it may become more of a "fill in the blanks exercise," especially if completed during busy tax seasons when they simply don't have the time to focus their attention on it. This, however, does not diminish their role in filing timely and accurate tax returns knowing that they will impact financial aid eligibility.

The most-important impact tax professionals have is on the timeliness of the tax return, which is needed to appropriately update the FAFSA. This can become a problem if a tax filing extension delays the disbursements of federal funds for financial aid to the colleges. Beyond the timing, certain transactions such as stock and bond redemptions, capital gains, retirement rollovers and changes in tax filing status may result in tax savings, but their timing may have a negative impact on financial aid eligibility. In these cases it makes sense for a financial aid consultant to confer with tax professionals to strategize about the pros and cons of tax savings versus and qualifying for need based financial aid.

Financial Planners, insurance agents, banks, and so on provide a broad array of financial services and products based on a family's financial resources, risk tolerance, age, and where they are in life relative to college and retirement savings. Their scope is not limited to paying for college but on meeting lifetime events and building long-term wealth and financial security. A well qualified financial planner should understand your financial needs during certain milestones of your life, but also be sensitive to how your financial strategies will impact the need for financial aid. Be sure to understand the basics about insurance, annuities, and mutual funds, but never feel pressured into making financial decisions about college financing without second opinions and advice from a tax professional and/or financial aid consultant.

Below are two personal cases that may help to reinforce the importance of understanding the role of financial planners:

Case 1:

I had a client that was qualified for need-based financial aid and a federal Pell Grant due to her low income and assets during the student's freshman year in college. The following year, she liquidated an annuity that she inherited and incurred a large taxable gain. She then took her proceeds to the local banker that sold her another annuity to reduce her reportable assets for financial aid purposes. Since he did not bother to explain the tax and financial aid consequences before the sale, my client made two costly mistakes: The first was that she incurred a large one-time taxable gain for which she could have deferred until after her son graduated. The second was that she took her proceeds to purchase another annuity that would make an immediate distribution each month for ten years until it is was depleted. The result was an increase in income and taxes and a loss of financial aid for the student's sophomore year, including the Pell grant. All this would have been avoided if she had sought the advice of a well-qualified financial aid consultant, tax professional, and financial planner.

Case 2:

I worked with a client on completing their financial forms whose family consisted of a mother who worked and was the primary source of income, her husband, the student's father, who was permanently disabled with a terminal illness, and their college-bound son. Although they had about $150,000 in savings that would impact their need-based aid, I worked with a well-qualified financial planner who explained the options for an annuity tailored to their situation and how they would impact the student's financial aid. The plan sheltered their assets while their son was in college knowing that the investments with high rates of return would be payable after his father's death. He passed after the student graduated, but his sheltered investment with a healthy financial gain became payable to his beneficiaries when it no longer would impact his need-based financial aid.

Family Law Attorneys

About one-third of my clients are from single parent families. What makes this challenging is understanding how the child support and/or alimony payments are structured in the divorce decree. If the divorce decree has already been consummated, there may be little that can be done to change it. If not, more beneficial terms and conditions related to child support and payments to increase financial aid can be addressed. This is when financial aid consultants can provide their expertise to family law attorneys to ensure that the terms and conditions of the legal decree address the student's financial aid eligibility for college. The consult may include several "what-if" scenarios, including custodial and non-custodial incomes and contributions, duration, and whether or not it will it will impact their financial need.

3. College Planning and Selection

College Planners and Coaches offer a wide array of college search, test preparation, and assessment tools to help students qualify for and select the best college matches. Some also offer financial aid advice, however, in-depth financial aid and college affordability recommendations may not be their area of expertise.

Financial Aid Night Presenters: Most high schools offer free college and financial aid night presentations from not-for-profit educational and lending organizations that provide information about college admissions, college costs and financing. These presentations are informative, but can only provide general information. Because this can be the first time that parents are confronted with this information, they may be easily discouraged when the facts about high costs and debt become a stark reality. That said, this should not lead parents to give up or limit free or fee paid advice to overcome this hurdle. Rather, it should be viewed as another resource to consider at the start of the college journey.

Guidance Counselors provide an expansive list of services to understand and support the student's needs in consideration of the high school's rules, educational standards and goals.

Because of the large student caseloads, guidance counselors often don't have sufficient time, expertise or are empowered to provide the most-comprehensive financial solutions to pay for college. Consequently, they may direct students to the Internet, attend college fairs, take campus tours and/or attend free presentations to gain additional insight about required forms and general ways to pay for college.

I have tremendous amount of respect for the hard work and the vast scope of responsibilities assumed by these dedicated professionals. However, their wide range of responsibilities often limit their ability to provide in-depth support to resolve each families' unique financial challenges. Between directing students in finding the right college and writing recommendation letters, staying focused on test preparation and the application process, there is insufficient time and expertise to address the complex financial issues that affect the entire process. This is where a qualified financial aid professional can fill in the gaps related to the more personal and challenging questions that arise to ensure the most appropriate path for college financing success. Here are some typical parental financial questions that guidance counselors may not be qualified or authorized to answer:

- What are the best loans for us to consider?
- How will the family's debt impact their ability to borrow for college?
- How do certain investments and ownership impact their expected family contributions?
- How much debt load can the family assume for other college bound siblings?
- What role will the non-custodial parent play in paying for college?
- What will it take to appeal a financial aid award?
- What is the return on investment for a college education?
- How will business income help or hurt financial need?
- How do you prepare a family budget?
- What are the best investments to pay for college?
- What financial aid questions should you ask on a campus visit?
- How do the tax laws reward families with college students?
- How do you legally defer income and assets?
- How does UTMA and UGMA accounts impact Expected Family Contribution?

- What are the different calculations for the FAFSA and CSS/ Financial Aid Profile?

4. College Resources

Campus Tour Guides will more than likely be the first people that parents and students will meet on campus. They are usually enthusiastic student ambassadors that accentuate the positive aspects of attending a specific school. They can provide exciting and interesting information about student life and the academic experience that the institution offers, but they are by no means the experts on all aspects of admission and financial aid. Parents and students should recognize that campus tours are akin to a warm-up, and they should prepare the full range of questions that should be asked during campus visits and during the time they spend speaking with other school representatives after the tour. For this reason, it is wise to review all of the available materials, including applications, financial aid information, brochures, etc., before a campus visit in order to perform an in-depth analysis of the institution in a more proactive manner.

Admissions Counselors are responsible for reviewing college applications, transcripts, test scores, essays, academic backgrounds, and activities, and an interview, if required, in consideration of their admissions standards and "enrollment management" policies. These policies that differ by college are used to target and recruit certain students to maintain and/or improve upon their profiles and rankings within the college community. Admissions offices are also responsible for awarding merit-based aid versus need-based aid, which goes through the financial aid department. Students need to be sensitive to the filing deadlines, requirements, and the differences and qualifications for need based and merit based financial aid.

Here are some questions to ask an admissions counselor:

- How do you decide on the candidates that are at the top of your recruitment lists?

- Why should I consider attending your college?

- How do you weigh a student's GPA and test scores in your admissions process?

- What is your retention rate?

- What is the biggest reason that students dropout?

- How does your study abroad program work?

- How do you determine your merit-based awards?

- How many students do employers recruit from your school after graduation?

- Can I attend classes and stay in your dorms to evaluate your school?

- How easy is it to enroll in a class before it is closed out?

Financial Aid Offices / Student Financial Services: College financial aid offices do a remarkable job managing and coordinating financial aid programs. Yet, there are mixed dynamics and a quality of service that is often dependent on the college and who answers the phone. Beyond the more experienced financial aid counselor, it is likely that a student or less experienced person may handle incoming calls to the office. If possible, visit the financial aid office to schedule a meeting with a financial aid counselor in order to ensure that any problem is resolved. Additionally, always get the name of the person that helped you. It's critical never to wait until the last minute to resolve any questions or concerns related to the college financial aid office!

Financial Aid Administrators

Financial Aid Administrators are responsible for the review, analysis and determination of need-based financial aid for college via the FAFSA data and other required forms. They package the financial aid awards using need-based formulas and criteria in addition to merit-based aid awarded by the admissions office which is adjusted for any outside scholarships. They also employ a process called

'Professional Judgment' in consideration of exceptional financial circumstances or award appeals. Additionally, they provide help completing forms, information about loans, payment plans, borrowing, and work-study programs.

Here are some questions to ask financial aid administrators:

- What is the Cost of Attendance and what does it include?
- Is the college "Need Blind" or "Need Aware"?
- How much of a family's unmet need is met?
- What are the average need-based and merit based awards?
- On average, how much debt is owed after graduation?
- How do you award federal work-study?
- What is your criteria for awarding need-based aid?
- How does Early Action or Early Decision impact financial aid?
- Do the financial aid packages include alternative or PLUS loans?
- What information is required to appeal an award?
- How do you qualify to become a Resident Assistant?

Bursar /Student Financial Services: A Bursar is an institutional financial administrator that manages student accounts and related financial responsibilities. They handle student billing, receivables and interface with lenders, installment payment plan providers, and scholarship administrators and work closely with financial aid and other departments when necessary. They may also send out tax statements such as form 1098-T, Tuition Statement and provide other financial services. Some institutions may also have a director of student financial services that provides similar and/or expanded services depending on their organizational structure.

College Advisors can help students to select majors, drop and add courses, resolve personal and academic problems, review academic progress and provide the resources to support college success. They can also help with resume development, transfer issues, problem solving and referrals to other academic and professional development services.

5. Government Agencies and Loan Sources

The US Department of Education processes federally funded loans including the Stafford, Perkins, and PLUS loans. They are responsible for loan entrance and exit counseling, loan deferments and forbearance and awarding additional Stafford loans to students whose parents have not been approved for a PLUS loan. This department also administers the FAFSA and provides documentation and support regarding financial aid, loan types, borrowing options, and related information.

State agencies also process loans and scholarship programs for public education and are based on standardized test scores, need and other criteria.

6. Other Services

Alternative Loan Services provide college loan funding to supplement any federal, state or college funding. These loans generally require a credit worthy co-signer since most students do not have an established credit history.

Installment Payment Plan Providers

These firms offer no interest payment plans in lieu of, or in addition to, any other funding sources. Some colleges may also offer similar plans or will direct students to the providers that do so for their school. Each plan can require a small up-front fee, usually less than $100, to designate a fixed dollar amount to be spread over multiple months without any interest. While this is not a loan or financial aid, it does offer a solution for those who wish to allocate some of their disposable income or savings to pay for college to lessen the need to borrow and incur interest expenses.

Test Preparation Services

Students may increase their SAT, ACT or other test scores by using a qualified test preparation service or tutor to learn test strategies, especially if they are used for admissions and merit-based aid at the colleges they are interested in. Families should be well aware of the importance of these scores relative to grades, class standing, and other factors that will impact student acceptance and school quality.

FAIR Test

The National Center for Fair and Open Testing[6] is a not-for-profit organization that strives to reduce the use of standardized tests as gatekeepers to higher education as colleges are reexamining their admissions policies and de-emphasizing test scores. This site also lists the colleges that do not require or those that make standardized testing optional.

---

6 http://www.fairtest.org/university

CHAPTER 4

Why Might You Need A Financial Aid Consultant?

"The speed of communications is wondrous to behold. It is also true that speed can multiply the distribution of information that we know to be untrue."

- Edward R. Murrow

Positive recognition and client retention as a financial aid professional is earned through hard work, service excellence and providing clients with value added benefits. Yet, financial aid consultants have often had to fend for themselves when providers and presenters of free services argue against paying for what can be done at no cost. Such suggestions only make sense as a warning to avoid scammers and those that fail to provide a high level of value added support. However, these arguments make little sense when a negative label is slapped onto a profession in which a few rotten apples spoil the bunch. That's why it makes sense to understand the other side of the argument to make a more rational decision.

Should You Pay To Have Your Taxes Prepared?

If the IRS doesn't warn taxpayers against buying tax preparation software or to use qualified tax preparers, why doesn't the U.S. Department of Education and educational institutions acknowledge the potential value of more that offer more personalized and in depth expertise and support to those who want to pursue it? The reason is simply because there is a greater focus on warnings about scholarship scams and access to free information and services than there is about knowing that there are other fee-based professional service providers that offer more personalized and in depth support for those that want to pursue it. Using fee-based services for tax filing and/or college financing are merely a matter of choice based upon desired levels of support and the sought after value they provide.

What Is A Financial Aid Consultant?

The best definition of a financial aid consultant is as follows:

> *Financial aid consultants help students and parents through the financial aid process by providing advice and assistance that <u>supplements</u> the services offered by the schools themselves. Just as some people seek out the services of a tax preparer for their income tax returns, a <u>competent</u> financial aid consultant can help a family navigate through the sometimes-confusing financial aid application process.*[7]

I underlined the words *supplements* and *competent* to accentuate the fact that these services do not replace, but rather, enhance those offered for free. Moreover, they should not be construed in a negative light if they provide more in depth and personalized strategic advice for which free resources generally neither have the time to provide nor the expertise of a competent financial aid consultant.

Why The First FAFSA Is Only A Prelude Of More To Come

Now, let's take a look at the number of forms or processing steps involved in the financial aid process. Keep in mind that these are just some of the time sensitive and not always straightforward forms and processing steps associated with the initial submissions, updates and other forms that families are likely to encounter.

---

7 http://www.finaid.org/scholarships/consultants.phtml

Form Processing Steps	
Document	Purpose
FAFSA https://fafsa.ed.gov	Initial Submission starting each January 1st
SAR https://fafsa.ed.gov	FAFSA output report (1)
FAFSA https://fafsa.ed.gov	College and other updates made as needed
SAR https://fafsa.ed.gov	FAFSA output report (2)
FAFSA https://fafsa.ed.gov	Tax Updates from completed tax returns.
SAR https://fafsa.ed.gov	FAFSA output report (3)
FAFSA https://fafsa.ed.gov	Taxes updates finalized from the actual IRS/Data Retrieval Download
SAR https://fafsa.ed.gov	Final FAFSA output report (4)
IRS/tax Transcript http://www.irs.gov/Individuals/Get-Transcript	Request this copy of your tax return when the IRS Data Retrieval Tool cannot be used to download tax data into the FAFSA
CSS/Financial Aid Profile https://student.college-board.org/css-financial-aid-profile	Required by some colleges using this more detailed form for institutional aid.
NCP/Profile https://ncprofile.college-board.com	Non-custodial parent completes this form when required by the college.
Verification	Required by the college for data to be audited.
IDOC (https://idoc.collegeboard.org)	Mail tax and related schedules to the IDOC, document imaging service when requested.
Actual Tax return	Send directly to college when required.
Financial Aid Award	Student and parental reviews and/or approvals are required before funds are disbursed.
Financial Aid Appeals	Appeal for more financial aid when warranted.
Stafford loan https://studentloans.gov	On-line Entrance Counseling and Master Promissory Note approvals are required for student loan disbursements.
PLUS loan request https://studentloans.gov	Master Promissory Note is required for parental PLUS loan disbursements.
Alternative Loan Request(s)	Research and apply for non-governmental loans.
Installment payment plan	Periodic no interest payment plans to spread designated payments over multiple months.

Reading Between The Lines

Recently I came across the following information about financial aid consultants on the Big Future section of the College Board website.[8] While I respect what was written, I take issue with the facts that can be misleading. Here are some excerpts from this section along with some of my comments:

Free advice is available.

- **Families who feel uncomfortable with the financial aid process may turn to consultants for help. <u>Many of these consultants offer legitimate services. Even so, hiring a consultant is usually not a good idea.</u>**

Hiring a consultant that <u>offers legitimate services</u> is an option and a choice for which parents are paying for specialized expertise and analytical abilities that can result in a great return on a small investment. "<u>Usually not a good idea</u>" does not mean always. It depends upon finding the best service providers that can do more than just complete forms and waste valuable time.

- **Free advice is available. Consultants charge a fee for <u>advice you can get for free from high school counselors and college financial aid officers.</u>**

Free advice is definitely available. While there is an abundance of free advice, there is a scarcity of personalized and in depth analytical support from those with experience and a scope of knowledge that is not limited to the institution or agency providing it. High school and college counselors also have a diverse array of responsibilities that limit the time that they can spend with each student. They can only make recommendations and are not empowered to probe into a family's financial resources and credit worthiness or make college financial decisions on their behalf.

---

8 https://bigfuture.collegeboard.org/pay-for-college/grants-and-scholarships/how-to-avoid-financial-aid-scams.

- **Consultants may not get you more. It is <u>unlikely that a consultant can get you more financial aid than you can get yourself.</u> Financial aid officers make decisions based on formulas and consultants cannot change the numbers for your family.**

Consultants are not focused on formulas or trying to change them. They provide sound financial advice in consideration of income and assets and the best strategies for managing costs and lowering expenses. Their thinking is much broader than the results of a form. Personally, I also advise about the financial aid appeal and professional judgment process and offer to help craft an effective appeal letter.

- **<u>Some advice is bad.</u> Untrustworthy consultants might suggest moving money around or buying something expensive so it looks like you have less cash. Financial aid officers spot these tricks easily. If they suspect you of being dishonest, they might reject your financial aid application.**

Although I would not personally offer specific investment advice, I would refer a client to a qualified financial planner who could offer them more appropriate choices. Moving money around or buying something expensive without considering liquidity, impact, and costs, as well as long term financial planning makes little sense when parental assets are not factored into the FAFSA calculation as heavily as is income. Such a strategy should not be indicative of what a more seasoned and objective financial aid professional should suggest.

- **Some consulting services are scams. Some of these services make misleading promises and false guarantees in order to get your money and financial information.**

I agree that the buyer should always be aware of scams and misleading statements, which is why it is important to know what to look for in terms of the quality, experience, and reputation of the services that they provide.

All Buyers Should Be Aware

Scam artists and opportunists can take advantage of vulnerable clients. Thus, buyers should be better informed as to the many pitfalls they can encounter when seeking professional guidance in these matters. They should heed warnings about avoiding scholarship scams, paying a high price for the mechanical act of filling in the blanks of a financial aid form with no additional follow-up support, or paying for expensive services that generate more paper and information that most families don't need or can handle.

The bottom line is that finding quality professional financial aid support all depends on four very important factors:

1. The level of expertise and experience of the service provider.

2. The value added services that extend beyond just completing a form.

3. The professional integrity of the service provider.

4. Fees for these services.

Should You Attend Free Financial Aid Presentations?

Of course you should. I've found that much of what can be learned is less from the presentations and more from the questions that parents ask and the quality of the answers. These are the questions about the cost, contracts, and the scope of the services not always discussed in detail within the formal presentation.

The thing that concerns me with regard to free financial aid workshops is when they aim to lure angst-ridden parents to agree to a free initial consultation. This leads to individuals feeling pressured into committing to more costly contracts and long term services that may not be necessary or affordable.

With this in mind, parents should give careful consideration to which services to pursue without being told what they may or may not need. There are reputable companies that offer value added services with a specific focus on affording a college education. They can be found through referrals from parents, other respected professionals and by networking with college students that have worked with consultants with proven track records and positive results.

Case Study: Financial Aid Consultants To Avoid

I had a colleague with a strong sales background that became affiliated with an organization that provided financial aid services similar to what I just described. He was conscientious yet inexperienced in the financial aid consulting field, so he asked me to sit in on one of his counseling sessions to critique his services.

Throughout the session I noticed that he asked the parents many scripted financial questions, which he entered into a computer program that was networked with the organization with which he shared his profits and generated reports. Despite the lengthy report output, his advice was to take a home equity loan to pay for college. He then provided these parents with a book about college funding that he did not write but had paid to have his name printed on it as its author. This is an example of a sales job that doesn't cut it, especially for parents that couldn't afford to pay a high price for expertise and creative and viable solutions that were not provided.

Even though these services may have been informative, they did not provide any real value, nor was this colleague qualified to call himself an expert in the matters he was providing such help. Even his book was a facade that was neither original nor honest.

As a postscript, he finally gave up this business less than a year after he started. It just didn't work out!

Who Can Afford Financial Aid Consultants?

- **Families that have the financial means to pay for extensive college planning** and dealing with the other services are fortunate to be able to do so and factor these services into their college budget.

- **Families with low incomes** on the other hand should take advantage of the free services if their forms are relatively simple and choices more limiting. Fee-paid services may be needed if special circumstances need for privacy and complex financial scenarios prevail.

- But what about the **vast population of middle class families** that are caught in between when it comes to qualifying for financial aid and seeking more affordable college options? They don't need the expensive but reasonably priced support to accomplish their goals.

This is why my business model is focused on charging affordable fees to build customer retention and provide the services to get their child through college. Let's take a look at what I do.

When considering any financial aid consultant, parents should be aware of the services that they will provide. An example of my services are listed on my website at www.financialaidconsulting.com and included on the folllowing pages to provide an idea of what should be expected from a financial aid consultant:

College Planning

- Helping students establish criteria for researching colleges.
- Preparing for campus visits.
- Spreadsheet analytics.
- Scholarship searching.
- Exploring 4-year college alternatives.

Financial Aid Forms

- Preparation
- Analysis
- Tax Updates
- Analysis of prior years' forms.
- Expected Family Contribution review.
- "What If" Scenarios.
- Scheduling and follow-up.

Financial Aid Award Analysis

- Understanding what it means.
- Evaluating the available options.
- Crunching the numbers.

Writing Powerful Appeal Letters

- Defining what is needed.
- Effectively presenting the case.
- Remaining positive.

Scholarship Searches

- Brainstorming sources.
- Taking action.
- Reaping the benefits.

Reducing Anxiety

- Overcoming the fear of the unknown.
- Improving family communications.
- Clarifying financial responsibilities.
- Exploring alternatives.

Staying Organized and In Control

- Timetables
- Spreadsheet Analysis
- Progressive review and follow up.

What Questions Should You Ask A Financial Aid Consultant?

- What is your approach to satisfying my requirements?
- What is your professional background?

- Where is a good meeting location (Office, phone, virtual)?
- What are your fees (fixed, hourly, contractual)?
- How many years do you have in the profession?
- What are your services?
- Can you provide referrals?

What Is Free Advice Worth?

It was once said that, *"free advice is worth what you pay for it."*

The good news is that there is a lot and sometimes too much of the same thing. The bad news is that it can lead to an information overload and redundancy. Contributing to this are other free services associated within high school and community outreach programs that do a nice job helping students. However, they may be limited in their financial expertise, as to what they can recommend, and the time that they can commit to the larger populations that they serve.

Even with this wealth of information, none of it will provide the peace of mind, support or expertise that can quell emotional angst, keep you on track, or lead to the logical steps for financing a college education. With this in mind it is important to decide if the free advice will satisfy your needs and ask "*so what*?" does this all mean?

Can You Pass The "So What?" Test?

As I think of all these free tools, I recall some great advice from a career counselor who taught me about the *So What? Test*. In essence, the test was about taking past accomplishments and asking, "So what would they mean to a future employer?" Rather than being stuck in the past, I had to look forward to what I could do or the value that I could provide.

The FAFSA, CSS/Financial Aid Profile and every other financial aid form is not so much a means to judge wealth or hardship but an opportunity to apply the "so what" test of what they report before deciding on the next steps. This is the big difference between the free and the do-it-yourself approaches versus professional, fee based support that can provide the best answers to the "so what?" test.

CHAPTER 5

How Do You Avoid Your Own Horror Story?

"It's better to keep your mouth shut and appear stupid than open it and remove all doubt."

- Mark Twain

N o one is immune to simple errors. Mistakes can, and often will, occur because of bad assumptions and undetectable changes throughout any complex process. As the journey of preparing financially for college is full of potential pitfalls and complications, the following case studies help illustrate how emotional decision-making, and uncertainty, as described in chapter 2, can impact financial aid and what you can do about it:

Missing The Point

While completing the FAFSA form of a student I volunteered to help, I hit a roadblock because of her mother's reluctance to provide her financial information. I respected her concern for privacy, but was not entirely comfortable with the decision, given the position she was in to complete the FAFSA without further support.

Regardless, several months passed until our next meeting. Upon asking her how things were proceeding with her college decision-making process, she said that she was happy to be accepted to her college of choice but was disappointed that she did not receive the financial aid award for which she thought she would be entitled.

Although I knew how guarded her mother was with her information, I offered to review her FAFSA to identify any potential errors that may have impacted her award. I discovered that instead of rounding most of her numbers up or down to the nearest dollar, she reported them in whole dollars including the cents after the decimal point. As a result, the $3,570.25 that should have been rounded to $3,570 was reported as $357,025 while $500.00 was similarly reported as $50,000, and so on.

After notifying the college about what had happened and correcting the errors, the student was grateful to receive a revised, and much more generous financial aid package that helped pave the way to a more affordable college education.

Lesson Learned: Be accurate, but don't be afraid to question anything that looks wrong.

Same Time Next Year

I was working with a client who was nervous about her daughter's CSS Financial Aid Profile that she submitted on her own and requested my professional advice to review what she had done. Her daughter was applying Early Decision for the 2012-2013 academic year to a college with a November 1, 2011 filing deadline. Because she wanted to get a jump-start on the financial aid process, she completed it in June 2011.

After assessing her request, I realized that it was impossible for her to complete that form for the upcoming academic year in June 2011 since it was not yet available until October 1, 2011. Before that, the only CSS/Financial Aid form available in June 2011 would be for the current 2011-2012 academic year that was already in progress and nearly over. In effect, the proper form for the correct year was never submitted!

Trying to submit a form too early is just as bad as not submitting one at all. Once we understood the problem, I helped her to prepare an accurate and timely form for the 2012-2013 academic year when it was available on October 1, 2011 in time to be considered for financial aid.

Lesson Learned: Despite the good intent, this problem could have been avoided if the client had paid more attention to detail and/or gotten the professional support to complete the correct form in the first place.

College Hits A Sour Note

Another family had a student whose heart was set on attending an expensive private college to obtain a degree in entertainment management. His father had little in savings and decided to liquidate his retirement nest egg to enable him to attend the school of his dreams. His father had also taken a parent PLUS loan to cover the unmet financial need knowing that it did not have to be repaid for several years.

While his father kept open lines of communication with his son, he never saw his grades nor maintained any regular correspondence since most of it was sent directly to him on-line. After the conclusion of the second semester, his father received disturbing news from the college: it appeared that his son had enjoyed college so much that he put little effort into his studies and had flunked out.

In the end, not only was the year wasted, but the father's retirement fund was depleted and he was saddled with parent loans that could no longer be deferred.

Lesson Learned: Despite the father's good intentions, his son was not accountable to his father and not financially responsible for the financial risks if he should fail. Paying for college is a partnership for which responsibility and accountability between parent and student is assumed. Although the father did all that he could to make the right decisions, he should have been more prudent knowing the financial risk of his kindness.

A word of advice: As a parent paying for college, make an agreement with the student that they will allow you to monitor their grades through the school's on-line system. Don't get caught off guard!

Scholarship Is Too Good To Be True

I helped a student who was, at the time, being raised by his grand-parents, both of whom had low fixed incomes and had poor credit. The student wanted to pursue a career in creating video games and was advised to apply to several for-profit colleges that offered that major.

When I reached out to help him, he had no idea what programs were available, what salaries and job prospects were for his prospective major beyond graduation, or how much it would cost to attend the out of state schools for which he was interested.

Several weeks later, we met again when he was happy to inform me that he was accepted into a for-profit program and received a $5,000 scholarship if he enrolled within the next two weeks. Although I did not want disappoint him, I knew that the $5,000 was a marketing tool used to entice students and would likely lead to a high price tag down the road that was beyond this family's financial capacities. To ease the pain and set the student on a more realistic course, I called his grandparents, who were, unfortunately, vague on the details.

Since they had little money, poor credit and were not prepared to co-sign or take on a loan for $25,000 they were happy I called. Though they wanted to do what was best for their grandson, they also wanted to know the facts. Although, it was disappointing and may have been a good program, the student moved on to a two-year program at a community college and transferred to a state college where he received his bachelors' degree in a related field with little to no debt and a bright future.

Lesson learned: Scholarships are not just awarded but earned. Students need to know the costs and benefits associated with their educational choices while understanding that some offers are simply too good to be true.

Parenthood Not Apparent

Jay lived at home with his two parents who had never legally married. His mother earned $15,000 per year working in the public school system while his father's salary was in the $65,000 range. Because Jay wanted to maximize his financial aid, he reported his mother's marital status on the FAFSA as "Never Married" although he lived with both parents.

Because his reported family income was low and there were other factors that were being questioned, his FAFSA was selected for a process called *Verification*. Upon verification of the names of all family members living at home, the marital status on his FAFSA had to be changed to "Unmarried and Both Parents Living Together" so that his father's income would be added to the FAFSA. This eliminated any consideration for a Pell Grant and forced the family to send the student to a more affordable community college

Lesson Learned: It is easier and less embarrassing to to be honest and understand all of the questions than to create a simple and embarrassing error that can prove costly.

Double Trouble

John was planning to attend a private university that required both a FAFSA and CSS Profile. His father was an only child and did whatever he could to help his elderly mother who was ready to move into an assisted living complex. Although the complex would assume full responsibility for her care, meals, medical help, and other amenities, it also required that she sign her assets over to them for lifetime care. She decided that the best way to handle this was to transfer only $100,000 of her assets to the complex. She kept her remaining $350,000 in assets "hidden" by having her son manage it under his name and social security number rather than assigning it to the assisted living complex. She would then draw upon her funds when needed and any remainder would be his after her death.

John's father invested wisely and earned a substantial amount of interest on the $350,000 that he was safekeeping. At year-end, he received an IRS form 1099-INT with reportable interest income on grandmother's hidden nest egg that was reported on his tax return.

While completing John's financial aid forms, his parental income was low and allowed him to qualify for need-based aid, until I came to the asset section, which included his grandmother's assets that were now owned, managed and reported under his father's social security number. The parents argued that the $350,000 was actually the grandmother's asset that they were holding for her until she died. Even so, the assets and income were in John's father's name and social security number and thus, includable in the financial aid calculations, regardless of their intended use. The result was a significant increase in the family's EFC and a reduction in financial aid.

Lesson learned: It is not advisable to hide someone else's assets and reduce financial need by not reporting them. Financial planning would have provided better options for managing these funds.

This Is Not Big Business

Karen's parents owned a sole proprietorship with a net equity of $500,000. It was an S Corp with five employees for which their net business income was reported on their Form 1040. When they completed their FAFSA, they included the value of the business as a parental asset that resulted in a significant increase in their EFC or "Expected Family Contribution" and a decrease in their need for financial aid. To make matters worse, they had sustained a significant decrease in business income and sought my help to review their FAFSA and do whatever was necessary to increase Karen's financial aid award.

After reviewing Karen's FAFSA, I recognized that the value of a business with less than 100 employees should not have been reported as a parental asset on the FAFSA. I then corrected Karen's FAFSA by reducing their business value from $500,000 to 0 to significantly lower their EFC and increase Karen's financial need for college.

Lesson learned: By understanding each question on the FAFSA, the risk of errors to calculate financial aid can be reduced. For this reason, attention to detail is so important for maximizing the financial aid award ultimately obtained for families.

Giving Them Credit

Faye and Ben had lost their jobs during the real estate meltdown. They were unable to refinance their home and had resorted to using their credit card to pay for everything until they could secure new employment. After two years, they found employment with combined incomes of $200,000 before their son, was applying to college. This increased their Expected Family Contribution and reduced their need-based financial aid.

Because they had amassed over $225,000 in credit card debt that was not factored into the FAFSA calculations, I wrote an appeal letter. In it, I explained how normal living expenses and staggering credit card payments left them with poor credit and no means to borrow. These factors along with supporting documentation were taken into consideration and the appropriate financial aid was rewarded.

Lesson Learned: There are exceptions to the norm that can be appealed if they are well documented and presented. Incurring high credit card debt is not a good reason by itself or justification to merit additional financial aid. In this story, the client used credit as very expensive last resort to pay for normal living expenses while they were unemployed. It is of great benefit for parents to be able to recognize how to report and document exceptions like these knowing that their EFC calculation may not be accurate.

A Less Taxing Situation

Beth and Lenny provided me with their tax return to update their FAFSA after their daughter Ella's freshman year in college. After ensuring that their financial aid forms were accurately prepared, I noticed that they did not take advantage of the American Opportunity Tax Credit, which would have given them up to a $2,500 in federal tax credit.

The issue was that the college sends the IRS form 1098-T Tuition Statement, which has qualifying information for determining if the student's parents can take the credit, directly to the student. Since Ella did not know what it was for, she discarded it without informing her parents. Since there was no form and Beth and Lenny's tax preparer failed to ask if they had a college age student, they lost out on the credit.

After my review, I suggested that Ella contact her college to get another form 1098-T so that her parents could file an amended tax return to receive the credit. They were then able to file an amended tax return and receive the $2500 tax credit.

Lesson Learned: Students should be advised to provide their parents with any tax forms with which they are unfamiliar. Tax preparers should also be advised if there is a college age student that may qualify them for certain educational credits that can be used in many ways including paying for college.

Misdirected Interest

Another client got ill-conceived advice from someone that suggested that he take a home equity loan to reduce the value of his home and increase the need for financial aid. The client heeded their advice and took a $200,000 home equity loan. He then deposited the proceeds into his bank account so that he could earn interest on his money to pay for college and reduce the equity or asset value of his home.

What he failed to realize was that the value of his primary residence on which he took the loan did not need to be reported on the FAFSA form, yet the $200,000 on deposit did. This increased his Expected Family Contribution, resulted in higher interest expenses on the full $200,000 and yielded only a very small return on the low interest rate paid on his savings account.

I convinced him that it would be best to repay the home equity loan and consider a home equity line or other financing source in which he could use the money as needed. Fortunately my analysis was done well before the FAFSA was available so that he had sufficient time to do what was necessary to reduce the family's Expected Family Contribution without the $200,000 in reportable assets that were repaid.

Lesson Learned: Free advice is often worth what you pay for it. Although the general assumptions may work, it is best to evaluate the pros, cons, financial returns and expenses for each financial strategy in relation to its overall impact on financial aid eligibility.

NOTE: Everyone's situation is different. Please recognize that all of these "tales of woe" are examples of the experiences of others. Each reader should evaluate their own situation and consider taking it to a knowledgeable expert or consultant to fully evaluate what's their best options.

CHAPTER 6

Is A College Education Worth The Investment?

"An investment on knowledge pays the best interest"

\- Benjamin Franklin

The value of a college education is not solely based on either the college attended or major, but on how the student can use their formal educational and interpersonal skills to satisfy their career objectives and employer's needs.

Regardless of the college or major, most conscientious students will benefit from the learning and social experiences that lead to a college degree. It is also a good investment that provides a lifetime credential in the form of a degree, which will lead to generally higher compensation as compared to those that have made other choices.

The risks and rewards of attending any college will vary by the type of college, net price, and the projected supply and demand for the student's services upon graduation. Moreover, the cost of a college education is often extended beyond the four years because of financial and other needs. Some professions also require advanced degrees and unpaid internships and training that may lead to more lucrative long-term career paths but are substantially more expensive. Therefore the value of a college education should be determined based upon the long-term costs and lost income opportunities while in college in relation to the lifetime earnings potential and payback.

How About A Candid Discussion?

It's worthwhile to have a candid discussion with the student to address their academic standing, test scores, career interests, and criteria for selecting colleges. Moreover, they should be able to answer the question: Can you convince us how much we should pay for your college education and how much you plan to earn after graduation? These are fair and challenging questions that can only be answered with further research about the net price of each college, employment outlook, and pay scale projections, which are referenced later in this chapter.

Families should not be pressured into making the wrong decisions without evaluating their options, which may include, but are not limited to the following:

- State versus private colleges.
- Living on campus versus commuting.
- On-line degrees versus on campus programs.
- Full-time versus part-time degrees.
- Two-year versus four-year programs.
- Trade school versus college.
- Deferred admission.
- Gap year(s)
- The military.

All of this simply means that there are many options and creative ways to reduce the costs of a college education, even if it involves some sacrifice or inconvenience.

Understanding Investment Value

A college education is a unique investment that will have a significant impact on the family's financial resources. It can be both a great expense with limited or no payback, or a great investment. An example of an expense with little to no payback or investment value would be attending a school that doesn't provide the quality of education, the right majors, a positive learning environment and the support for the student to thrive and become marketable to potential employers. Ill-conceived and pressure-laden decisions for attending the wrong school can be a costly expense and a poor or negative long-term investment. This happens far too often when students drop out, transfer from other colleges, change majors or realize that they are just not interested in college. These are things that could be avoided with effective family communication coupled with objective professional advice.

Making the right choices will still incur an expense, but it will also provide a better investment in terms of a valuable degree that offers s lifetime of professional and financial opportunities. Like any good investment, families should perform their due diligence by being aware of each college's reputation, retention rates and post graduate job opportunities to understand the expected return on their investments. In this way, parents can gain peace of mind knowing where the degree will lead and have the confidence in their child's ability to achieve it.

Where Does College Fit Into The Picture?

College is a unique investment in that no model can accurately predict the rate of return, the personal wealth, the job satisfaction, or the overall happiness it will provide. A college degree is both a hard earned credential that offers a wealth of career opportunities and a source of cash flow for those that are ready and willing to pursue one. It may also be the wrong choice for students and well-intending parents that assume that college is the next or only step beyond high school without spending adequate time exploring the costs and potential end results.

This is why I cannot overemphasize the importance of researching career opportunities and compensation as a means of determining the end result or benefit of a college education. Although this does not guarantee future employment, it provides greater insights into which career fields will be in demand, salary ranges and required educational levels.

Questions To Ponder

- Why pursue a degree in social work or education at an expensive private college when the same degree can be pursued at a much less expensive public university?

- Is it worth pursuing an expensive engineering degree at a private college that may require substantial student loans but offer a larger starting salary?

- Why go to a four-year private college with a high acceptance rate when a two-year college and transfer to a state college may be a better choice?

- Why go to a four year college that does not provide co-operative education or real world learning versus strictly classroom training?

- How do the college placement office(s) and recruitment services help students obtain employment after graduation?

- Which career fields will pay the most after graduation?

- Which careers require advanced degrees?

The answers to these and any other questions can be found during campus visits, research, and effectively networking with students, alumni and faculty.

How Do You Predict The Future?

I invite you to check out the following resources that will answer questions related to career fields, salaries, college costs, and return on investments. This is one of the most important steps before the college search rather than after graduation. It will also serve to answer questions regarding if it is worthwhile to even pursue a college degree when a two year certificate or trade school program or apprenticeship can result in a well-paying position. Knowing the likelihood of success and projected salaries should help to decide which colleges provide the most affordable educations so that neither the student nor the parent are encumbered with substantial long-term debt or poor returns on their educational investments.

Here are some helpful websites to explore future careers that may be worth pursuing:

Salary.com
http://www.salary.com/Education/EducationResult.asp
Provides salary and job search and educational data to find jobs and compensation. It is a great site for identifying current job openings, what they require, and salaries.

Pay Scale
http://www.payscale.com
This website provides tools for performing both compensation and career related searches. It allows you to determine earnings potential before deciding on how much to spend on a college education. Some of its many features include: College Costs and Return on Investments; College salary reports; Career Research and Salary calculators

College Scoreboard
http://www.whitehouse.gov/issues/education/higher-education/college-score-card
This website can be used to find out more about a college's affordability and value so you can make more informed decisions about which college to attend.

Occupational Outlook Handbook
http://www.bls.gov/ooh/
One of the most comprehensive ways to research careers is offered on the US Department of Labor's website www.bls.gov/ooh/. It is a research tool to delve into employment data, statistics, occupational descriptions, requirements, median salary, education levels, job growth, number of new jobs, highest growing and occupational data descriptions. For example, searches can be made by

highest paying job, fastest growth, and most new jobs, median pay, projected growth.

<u>My Majors</u>
http://www.mymajors.com
My Majors offers a concise way to research majors, colleges, and careers. All it takes is completing a simple registration to match colleges, majors, and careers in several easy steps.

<u>US News and World Reports does a nice job ranking some of this data by job category</u>
http://money.usnews.com/careers/best-jobs/rankings.
This survey ranks and describes the best jobs by industry salary ranges, median salary, employment, and unemployment rates to provide a real world assessment of the job market demand and how much you can expect to earn.

CHAPTER 7

How Do You Make The Most Of Your Campus Visits?

The secret to getting ahead is getting started."

- Will Rogers, Autobiography, 1949

Campus visits provide a great opportunity to test drive which colleges are best to further a student's education. Unfortunately, students may get ahead of themselves by not establishing consistent evaluation criteria or having discussions as to whether the school is simply too expensive an option. This is why effectively planning a campus visit will save time, money, and focus the family's energy in the right direction.

Get The Facts-Plan Ahead

Students should schedule meetings with their guidance counselors and conduct independent research before summer vacation to learn more about which colleges to consider. They should also attempt to obtain the names of recent high school grads that are now in college and with whom they can network. As they establish their criteria, they should visit websites that offer further insight and opinions about selected colleges before deciding on where to visit. Sites such as http://nces.ed.gov/collegenavigator/, http://www.cappex.com, and http://www.collegeclicktv.com are good resources to get the process started.

Map out a travel plan to visit colleges en route to family vacation spots or plan day trips. Though colleges may not be in full session, you can learn a lot by walking around, observing and talking to people on campus who may be able to help provide more sufficient information later on in the college decision making process. The summer is also the least stressful period for students to work on a resume or a qualifications document and list of accomplishments that may be needed during a campus visit or interview.

When Should You Visit?

Once you have viable lists of colleges to explore, plan to visit a maximum of two per day within the same geographic area. This will allow ample time for each visit without parents or students burning out and losing interest. All too often, families travel long distances without documenting what they are evaluating or meeting with faculty and staff. It should be noted that adjectives such as: *Nice, Good, Too Large or Too Small,* and so on are weak critiques and should not be the only criteria that will result in a decision for the family to commit large sums of money to an institution.

What Is Your Evaluation Scorecard?

Both the parent and student should create separate spreadsheets to formulate their criteria for rating each campus visit. The following illustrates how they can be configured and then customized to meet any individual's needs.

The results are merely tools for discussion that are much more substantive than trying to judge a school by outside appearances or perfunctory information easily found in a brochure. Additionally, it may be worthwhile to take pictures of what was seen on the visit to compliment the rating charts, and request business cards whenever possible to maintain a record of individuals that can be reached if further contact is desired.

STUDENT CAMPUS EVALUATION SCORECARD

Student Rating (1-5)	Importance	School A	School B	School C
Majors	1	5	3	4
Student Teacher Ratio	2	3	4	3
Academic Support	3	3	4	3
Fraternities and Sororities	4	4	3	4
Work Study	5	2	5	3
Student Housing	6	5	4	3
Campus Layout	7	3	4	4
Fitness Facilities	8	4	5	3
Study Abroad Program	9	4	3	4
Social	10	2	3	4
Total Score		**35**	**38**	**35**

PARENTAL CAMPUS EVALUATION SCORECARD

Parents Rating (1-5)	Importance	School A	School B	School C
Net Costs	1	2	3	4
Payment plans	2	3	2	4
Campus Safety	3	2	5	4
Transportation costs	4	4	3	3
Counseling	5	4	4	4
Campus Housing	6	3	3	4
Off Campus Housing	7	5	3	3
Tutoring	8	4	2	2
Food Quality	9	4	3	4
Work Study	10	3	2	3
Total Score		**34**	**30**	**35**

This example shows both consistent and more widespread scoring of the 20 items listed. It also shows the relative importance of each of the criterion that can be used to come up with weighted averages or use more sophisticated statistical measures. Focus can be placed on the top scores (5) and low scores (1) for their relative importance. These scorecards are only tools for discussion meant for consistently evaluating all colleges in addition to a student's qualifications and likelihood of being accepted.

What Was My First Campus Visit Like?

My first campus visit was at a prestigious college populated by students from affluent families whose parents were captains of industry and the movers and shakers of the world. Everywhere I looked, I saw students with designer clothes driving fancy new cars while I drove onto campus with my beat up used car, faded polyester pants, and a few bucks in my wallet.

I used my evaluation spreadsheet and felt confident that I had the grades and intellect to succeed there. However, queasiness in my stomach and a pounding headache warned me that it was not the right fit. It was then that I decided to pursue my second college choice after having something to compare it to. That campus visit went much smoother, not because more students were dressed like me, but because it met my criteria and felt better knowing that it had had the type of students with whom I had something in common. It turned out to be the right choice both academically and professionally with a world-renowned co-operative education program that enabled me to gain practical business experience while graduating without any student debt.

How Do You Make The Most Of Your Visit?

Plan college visits to provide opportunities to question the tour guide. They are likely to be upbeat, satisfied students that will provide a cursory look at the campus but will, expectedly, not have all of the answers. Because of this, there may be general information sessions with various departments, deans or administrators, coaches (if applicable), and other departments that should be attended as needed. It may be helpful during these sessions for the student to have their transcripts, course descriptions, and a resume or portfolio of accomplishments to share and distinguish themselves from other candidates.

Both parents and students have different interests and should plan to leave ample time to roam the campus and check things out on their own. This is a healthy move especially as spending too much time together creates the potential for stress, which can turn a pleasant college visit into a strained and uncomfortable experience. This also provides a more effective way of comparing notes and covering more territory within a limited amount of time.

Plan to meet with admissions and financial aid counselors as well as alumni relations and career placement officers to learn about services. Additionally, make contact with those who are involved from the beginning to the end of the college experience to get a sense of the culture and social environment the student will interact with, and have to deal with when they attend college. Be sure to know as much as possible about the college before getting there and ask questions related to your Campus Evaluation Scorecard.

Parents and students should also ask questions about:

- Merit and need based aid qualification and statistics.
- Net costs.
- Financial aid appeal process.
- Student debt amounts after graduation.
- Majors offered and acceptance rates.
- Transfer and AP credits.
- Counseling support.
- Types of students targeted for admission.
- On-line and computer taught course offerings.
- Full-time faculty and teacher assistant taught courses.
- Average number of years to graduate.
- Dropout percentages and dropout reasons.
- Resident Assistant requirements and opportunities.
- Course and professor rating statistics.
- Placement services statistics.

Questions like these should focus on the quality and value of the education, graduation rates, financial aid awards and net costs and whether it is worth spending the money and incurring the debt to attend that college.

Students should mingle with regular and transfer students, eat at the student dining facilities, visit the library, student center, and bookstore, and attend classes both large and small. They should also network with students and arrange a follow-up trip to stay in the dorms and attend other classes. Additionally, they should look into part-time studies and working opportunities to reduce their expenses at the school and earn extra money.

Both students and parents should drive around campus and surrounding communities to discover the area, medical facilities, public safety, and the available transportation to return home to get a feel for the school's surrounding area and support services.

Thank You?

A common faux pas is that people fail to acknowledge a visit with a simple thank you note. Beyond the common courtesy of doing so, it is an effective way to thank those that have provided their time or services. It also helps a student stand out from those that did not take the time to do so. It may be included in an admissions file as a way to show the level of interest a student has in attending the school.

Keep in mind that thank you notes don't have to be long, oversentimental, or insincere. They can be as simple as the following example:

Sally Student
3 Eagle Rock Road
Canton, MA 02021

July 26, 2014

Dean Robert Johnson
School of Management
XYZ College
Boston, MA 02117

Dear Dean Johnson:

Thank you for the opportunity to meet with you on July 22, 2014 to discuss my qualifications as a candidate for the International Business program.

I am excited about the information that you shared and look forward to being considered for this program for the Class of 2018.

Sincerely,
Sally Student

CHAPTER 8

Do You Have The Time To Invest?

"...It's not how much money you make, but how much money you keep, how hard it works for you, and how many generations you keep it for."

- Robert Kiyosaki

Each family's financial situation may seem similar but is, in reality, unique in terms of how they manage their money and prioritize their spending habits. Consequently, paying for college is a time consuming and critical task requiring effective financial and tax planning strategies.

What Is FAIT?

Paying for college is also a multi-dimensional process, which can best be described by FAIT. This is an acronym I've created to distinguish the broader financial aspects of paying for college. Unlike the word Fate, which describes the events that are out of our control, FAIT is just the opposite. FAIT is what you can control when you better understand the meaning and relevance of its components.

The **F** (Financing College) consists of **A** (Asset Management), **I** (income and Investment strategies), and **T** (Tax Ramifications). FAIT simply means that each financial decision will have a different benefit and impact on paying for college, and qualifying for financial aid. This is why it's so important to understand the benefits, shortcomings, risks, and rewards of the options available to families embarking on the college decision making process long before a financial aid form is submitted.

The following are a few examples of how FAIT can impact financial aid:

Assets

The FAFSA assesses certain parental assets such as savings, investments, second homes and so on at only 5.64% after allowances yet 20% for student owned assets without any offsetting allowances. Knowing these facts should help families to strategize about asset ownership and disposition in relation to how these transactions will impact their eligibility for need based financial aid.

Investments

Tax sheltered investments such as annuities are excluded from the FAFSA calculations but limit a family's cash to pay for college or meet other financial needs. Before purchasing any tax sheltered investments, families should analyze if sheltering these assets during the college years and beyond will significantly increase their need for financial aid and if the overall net returns on these investments are greater than the long term costs of borrowing to pay for college.

Income

Earning as much as possible will provide more financial resources to a family but should not be forsaken to potentially obtain more financial aid. Question whether it makes sense to lower a business's income to save on taxes and increase financial need for college or keep it high for growth and future borrowing. What may make sense is deferring income, bonuses, etc. into another tax year, but decide whether if it is worth giving it up for the opportunity to get more financial aid. This is where the old adage—*A bird in the hand is worth two in the bush* may make sense since having the money in hand is much cheaper than having to borrow it.

Taxes

Parents with Adjusted Gross Incomes of less than $24,000 may qualify for a Zero Expected Family Contribution if they file or are eligible to file a form 1040A or 1040EZ and meet certain, other qualifications. They may not derive this benefit if their tax preparer files a form 1040 and is unaware that the parents were eligible to file the other types of tax returns.

Parents with Adjusted Gross Incomes of $49,999 or less may qualify for the Simplified Needs Test. In this case, assets are excluded from the Expected Family Contribution if parents filed or are eligible to file a form 1040A or 1040EZ and meet certain other qualifications. But what if they filed a form 1040 and did not realize they were eligible for the asset exclusion?

As you can see, FAIT is really in your hands when it comes to making the right decisions.

How Much Time Do You Have?

A student's senior year of high school is what I like to call the *final lap* of coping with college costs. Once the initial sticker shock of a college education has been acknowledged, parents can look forward to the best options that are currently available to them and not lament about what could have been done to better prepare for the financial burden ahead.

There should be ample time for students and parents to seek scholarships, research college costs, project net costs, and Expected Family Contributions to get onto the right path. This is something that I do for all of my clients as it ensures that they don't receive last minute surprises or feel any undue stress.

The following table illustrates why it is never too late for parents and students to start planning and become proactive about the available college options they have rather than reactive to the costs of higher education:

Tax Year	Tax Year Starts	Tax Year Ends	2015-2016 FAFSA Available	Normal School Start
Dates	January 1, 2014	December 31, 2014	January 1, 2014	September 1, 2015
Timespans	1	11	1	8
Accumulative Months	1	12	13	21

General Timing Facts

- Financial aid forms cover a broader time period of about two years in which strategic financial decisions can be made.

- Asset reporting is based on <u>current</u> market and/or net values depending on which financial aid form is used and when the financial aid forms are prepared.

- The FAFSA requires certain income tax return data from the year <u>before</u> the student starts college.

- The CSS/Financial Aid Profile includes more information that can increase or lower your Expected Family Contribution based on a different set of formulas. It is always best to identify which colleges require this form during the college selection process. A List of participating colleges can be found at: https://profile-online.collegeboard.org/prf/PXRemotePartInstitutionServlet/PXRemotePartInstitutionServlet.srv

- Exceptions and special circumstances can also be reported to the college between when the FAFSA was submitted and when the student attends college.

What Are Some Of The College Related Investments?

529 Plans

529 plans (qualified tuition programs) that include College Savings Plans and Prepaid Tuition Plans are authorized by the federal government and sponsored by state agencies and educational institutions to encourage parents to save for college.

College Savings Plans

Earnings, dividends, capital gains and interest remain tax-free if used for qualified educational expenses in various types of colleges, community colleges, and trade and career schools. Each plan has an owner, normally the parent (although anyone can purchase the plan), for a designated beneficiary that can be changed over the lifetime of the account. Plans also require an administrator within the state or educational institution and plan managers that are normally mutual fund managers. Specific details regarding how the plans work, investment options and performance, fees, and other details should be inquired upon before making your investment decisions.

Prepaid Tuition Plans

These plans allow the buyer to purchase tuitions at current costs. Less than 20% of the states now offer these plans that have greater enrollment limitations. Check with your state educational authority for details and availabilities.

Here are the differences between both plans:

Provisions	College Savings Plans	Pre-Paid Tuition Plans
Tuition Lock	No	Yes
Coverage	Quailed expenses limited to investment value	Mostly tuition and mandatory fees
Age /Grade Limit	No Age Limits	Yes
Contribution Limits	Some have contribution limits	Lump and installment payments prior to purchase
State Guarantees	None	Some

Advantages And Disadvantages Of 529 Plans

Advantages:

- Doesn't require a large investment.

- Can be used for other beneficiaries if needed.

- Considered a parental asset (lower EFC assessment).

- Can be purchased from other states.

- Earnings are not taxable if used for qualified education expenses.
- Can be purchased by anyone.
- Purchaser can be the beneficiary.
- Multiple investment strategies.

Disadvantages:
- May not cover all costs.
- Can only change investments annually.
- Only used for qualified education expenses.
- Subject to penalty if not used for qualified education expenses.
- Tax benefits vary by state and residency.
- No guarantee or protection of investment.
- State of residency may not offer the best plan.

Coverdell Education Savings Accounts

These accounts only offer a modest $2,000 per year limit per beneficiary and are subject to a contribution phase out. This applies to single tax filers earning between $95,000 to $110,000 and joint filers earning between $190,000 and $220,000. Unlike a 529 plan, the account owner has greater flexibility for allocating their money though contributions must stop when the child turns 18. Funds can be rolled over to another family beneficiary if not used for qualified educational expenses before that beneficiary or family member reaches age 30. Then, the funds must be liquidated and subject to a non-qualified distribution.

Advantages:
- Investment flexibility.
- Can supplement 529 plans.
- Can also be used for certain K1-K12 expenses.
- Lower cost option than 529 plans.

Disadvantages:

- Limited contribution amounts.
- Income phase out for higher wage earners.
- May be "too little, too late."
- Must be used by age 30.

Series EE Bonds

U.S. Savings Bonds purchased after 1989 to help pay for qualified higher education Expenses College may be completely tax-free. However, the exclusion phases out for single tax filers earning between $74,000 and $89,700, and for joint tax filers earning between up to $112, 050 and $142,050. Maximum bond investments are $10,000 face value per owner, per type and per year. Withdrawals for non-qualifying expenses are taxable but not subject to penalty. Visit http://www.treasurydirect.gov/forms/savpdp0051.pdf for further information.

Uniform Gifts To Minors (UGMA) And Uniform Transfers To Minors (UTMA)

Uniform Gifts to Minors and Uniform Transfers to Minors are custodial accounts established for minor children for which the parents have control. However, income is paid at a lower, child's tax rate. This could be a good way to pay for college but will have an adverse impact on need-based aid. This is because the child gains control over the assets when they reach their age of maturity (usually between 18 and 21). Then these assets, for FAFSA purposes, are assessed at the student's 20% versus the parent's 5.64% rate. This, however, is a source of college funding that does not have to be borrowed subject to high interest rates.

Life Insurance

Life insurance is a good way of providing for an individual's family upon death. This can include paying for college or paying off student loans. It can also be a source for borrowing depending on the type of policy. Life insurance can range from basic coverage in the form of a very inexpensive term life policy or a more robust, whole life policy that offers other borrowing provisions. You can learn more about insurance by visiting http://www.einsurance.com/about/ and by meeting with a qualified agent that can tailor a plan to meet an individual's objectives. Term life insurance may also be an inexpensive a way for repaying student loan debt if a parent or student succumbs during the repayment period.

Other Investments—Meeting Of The Minds

This is not meant to be an extensive list or description of all of the investments to pay for college, but some of the many to consider. The purchase and sale of stocks, bonds, municipal funds, and others are many of the broader types of investment vehicles that incur different risk tolerances and investment strategies. They should be discussed with professionals that can address when it is most advantageous to maximize returns while being mindful of how they can impact financial aid.

CHAPTER 9

What's The Deal With Completing Financial Aid Forms?

"Lack of direction, not lack of time, is the problem. We all have twenty-four hour days."

- Zig Ziglar

What Should I Know About The Financial Aid Forms?

Completing a financial aid form is the starting point of a much longer and challenging journey before and after financial aid is awarded. That is why it should not be undertaken as a solo adventure knowing the financial risks and rewards that are at stake.

How Can Simple Mistakes Be Costly?

Financial aid forms processing cannot perform a 100% verification of the sources of your data or prevent the red flags that colleges may raise to question your submissions. They are not about if you can, but whether you should complete your financial aid forms on your own without professional expertise and support knowing how the risk of errors and uncertainty about taking the right next steps will impact college affordability. Then, when the reality sets in, it is time to question how much would you really save in actual dollars and lost opportunities if you were to complete these forms on your own.

Which Financial Aid Forms Are Required?

These are the four primary forms for need-based financial aid:

Form Name	Web Sites	Required By	Available	Cost
FAFSA	https://fafsa. ed.gov/FAFSA/ app/fafsa	All Colleges	January 1st	Free
CSS /Financial Aid Profile	http://student. collegeboard.org/ css-financial- aid-profile	Some private and state colleges	October 1st	$9 plus $16 per college
College's Own Forms	College Financial Aid Office	Some Colleges	Variable	Free
NCP /Non Custodial Parent Profile	https://ncprofile. collegeboard.com	Some private and state colleges	October 1st	$25

The **FAFSA (Free Application For Student Financial Aid)** uses a Federal Methodology formula to calculate Expected Family Contribution for federally need based financial aid.

The **CSS /Financial Aid Profile** uses a more extensive Institutional Methodology for funds that are controlled by certain colleges. A small group of colleges also use a Consensus Approach formula to diminish or eliminate the divergent results of need-based awarding of financial aid. More information about this program can be found at http://568group.org/methodology/

College Forms are also sometimes used for additional data that may not have been reported.

The Non Custodial Profile (NCP) is an on-line application designed to be completed independently by the non-custodial parent to determine the extent of financial support they can contribute to the student's education.

Who Is Eligible For The FAFSA?

https://studentaid.ed.gov/eligibility/infographic-accessible

Most students are eligible to receive financial aid by meeting the following requirements:

- High school diploma, GED or state approved home-schooled program.
- Regular student in an eligible degree or certificate program.
- Registered with Selective Service, if a male between the ages of 18 and 25.
- Have a valid social security number.
- Not in default of a federal student loan.
- Uses federal aid for educational purposes.
- Maintains satisfactory academic progress.
- U.S Citizen or U.S. National.

In addition to:

- US Citizen or National or have a green card Form I-551, I-151 or I 551 C.
- I-94 Arrival Departure meeting certain qualifications.

What Is The Timeframe For The FAFSA?

Each year on January 1st, the FAFSA becomes available for the upcoming academic year. That year begins on July 1st and ends the following June 30th. It's best to submit a FAFSA as close to January 1st as possible to lock in an early submission date and improve the chances for more need-based financial aid

Example: A FAFSA for all college students is available on January 1, 2015 for the 2015-2016 academic year. The academic year, for FAFSA purposes, begins July 1, 2015 and ends June 30, 2016.

How Does The FAFSA Work?

A FAFSA is the required ticket that opens the door to need-based financial aid, including an unsubsidized Stafford loan at the very least. It does this by calculating the EFC, (Expected Family

Contribution), or the minimum amount that a family can (but may not be able to) contribute to the cost of college.

- **The FAFSA Report** is the initial unedited input document that provides information to verify when it was submitted, Expected Family Contribution, Pell Grant Eligibility and other information before the edited data is available.

- **SAR (Student Aid Report)** is the edited output report after the FAFSA is processed. It is available to the student and electronically sent to each college. It's most important feature is the first page, which reports the submission and processing dates as well as the family's EFC. It also includes – '*Comments About Your information,*' such as: if your FAFSA has been selected for the verification, editing exceptions, and reminders to correct the FAFSA with actual tax return data. Verification is done randomly or based on selective criteria.

The **EFC, Expected Family Contribution** is derived from detailed calculations based on a family's income and certain assets and demographics that vary by state, family size, number in college, etc. Unlike the CSS/Financial Aid Profile, the FAFSA reports income for the last tax return year before the student starts each academic year.

Example: Tax return data for the 2014 tax year is used as the basis for financial aid for the 2015-2016 academic year using projected estimates. It is then finalized when the FAFSA is updated with an individual's actual tax return data retrieved from the IRS. The CSS / Financial Aid Profile for the 2015 / 2016 academic year will require tax data from 2014 (actual); 2015 (estimated or actual line by line detail) and 2016 (projected) income to look at a broader period of time.

The financial aid office at each college then deducts the Expected Family Contribution from their Cost of Attendance to determine the amount of unmet financial need that the college will attempt to fill with scholarships, grants, loans, and work-study.

How Does The FAFSA Calculate Your Expected Family Contribution?

The FAFSA is driven by a series of calculations based on such things as incomes, certain assets, family size, state of residency, taxes paid, employment expenses, parental age, number in college, etc. In turn, the required data and basis for calculating a family's Expected Family Contribution is reduced by certain allowances and offsets to determine the net amount to which the formulas would be applied.

How Does Marital Status Impact The FAFSA?

It is imperative to understand the effect parental marital status has on determining the Expected Family Contribution:

- **If both custodial parents are married** to each other and living together, both parent's household incomes are reported.

- **If the custodial parent remarries**, both the custodial and step-parent's household income are reported.

- **If the custodial parents are not married to each other** but live in the same household, both parent's income must be reported.

- **If both parents were never married or are legally separated or divorced**, report the income of the parent the student lived with most during the last 12 months. If not, provide information about the parent who provided more financial support during the last 12 months, or during the most recent year that the student received their support.

- **Same Sex Couples**- Consistent with the Supreme Court decision holding Section 3 of the Defense of Marriage Act (DOMA) unconstitutional, same-sex couples must report their marital status as married if they were legally married in a state or other jurisdiction (foreign country) that permits same-sex marriage, without regard to where the couple resides.

- **Grandparents, foster parents, legal guardians, older brothers and sisters, aunts and uncles** are not considered parents unless they legally adopted the student.

How Does Income Impact Financial Aid?

Student and parental incomes are subject to different calculations. For the 2015-2016 academic year, a student can receive an income protection allowance of $6,310 in addition to allowances for taxes and certain parental low income adjustments that are excluded from their Expected Family Contribution. Anything over these amounts are assessed at 50% and included in the resulting Expected Family Contribution.

Calculations for the parental income component provide for more allowances for taxes paid, income protection, and employment expense allowances, but use a sliding scale from 22% to 47% of the remaining available income to calculate the parental income component of the Expected Family Contribution.

What Is The Difference Between Taxable And Household Incomes?

Even though parental taxable income on a federal tax return has been reduced by pre-tax elections, the FAFSA calculations include pre-tax retirement plan contributions, child support, and other types of untaxed income. The reason for this is that household income is derived from many sources regardless of taxability. Therefore, adding these taxable exclusions back into the calculations provides a more realistic way of factoring in family income without providing an unfair advantage to those who enjoy the tax savings.

How Do Assets Impact The FAFSA?

Plan ahead by knowing the tax and financial aid reporting consequences regarding whether the student or parent would come out ahead. For example, if parental income and/or assets, do not qualify for need based financial aid, taxability may be less than if they were in the child's name and have relatively no impact on financial need.

I've had clients that were discouraged by the fact that they were not eligible for more financial aid because the student had a $100,000 in assets that would increase the family's Expected Family Contribution. It is important to remember that it is better to have the money on hand to pay for college than having to borrow it.

Student Assets are assessed at a flat 20% rate on the FAFSA (25% on the CSS/Financial Aid Profile), which is why many deem it unwise to have assets in the student's name.

Parental Assets are only assessed at 5.64% after allowances that are built into the formula. Assets include such things as cash, savings, checking, non-tax sheltered investments, other property, etc. Bear in mind that 529 Plans are considered a parental asset even though the student, and any other family member, can reap the benefit of the investment. Excluded are: retirement and tax sheltered account investments, primary residences, cars, jewelry, and the value of small businesses with 100 or fewer full-time equivalent employees.

How Do You Hide Or Shelter Parental Assets?

When parents ask for ways to hide their assets for financial aid purposes, my first reaction is to advise them to stop using the word *hide*. I prefer the word *reposition* as a more viable financial strategy to possibly lower the EFC. The bottom line is that decisions to reposition or use certain assets to pay for college should not be impulsive. Rather, they need to be based on data and analysis from qualified financial professionals to leverage the benefits of using certain available assets to pay for college or repositioning them for future uses.

Automatic Zero And Simplified EFC Calculations Explained

The FAFSA uses two special formulas for calculating the Expected Family Contributions for low-income families for the 2015-2016 academic year.

The Automatic Zero EFC calculation maximizes financial need by making the Expected Family Contribution zero if the parental

Adjusted Gross Income for dependent students and for independent students and their spouses is $24,000 or less and they meet the eligibility requirements listed below.

The Simplified EFC formula reduces a family's Expected Family Contribution by excluding the value of their assets if the parental Adjusted Gross income for dependent students and for independent students and their spouses is $49,999 or less and they meet the same eligibility requirements listed below. This is beneficial to low income families if they have highly valued assets that would not have otherwise been excluded from the FAFSA calculations without this calculation.

This threshold applies to tax filers with an Adjusted Gross Income of $49,999 or less. For non tax filers, W-2 and any other earnings from work not included on the W-2 are used to determine eligibility.

Eligibility Requirements For The Automatic Zero EFC and Simplified EFC Calculations:

Income
Meets the $24,000 or less income threshold for the Automatic Zero EFC or the $49,999 or less income threshold for the Simplified EFC calculation and meets any one of the following criteria:

Benefit Programs
Any household member receives benefits from any of the means tested federal benefits programs. These include-Supplemental Security Income (SSI), Supplemental Nutrition Assistance Program (SNAP), the Free and Reduced Price Lunch Program, Special Supplemental Nutrition Program for Women Infants and Children (WIC) and/or the Temporary Assistance for Need families (TANF)

Tax Filing
Parents or independent students and spouses filed or were eligible to—

- File an IRS Form 1040A or 1040EZ

- Filed an IRS Form 1040 but were not required to do so

- Were not required to file any tax return

<u>Employment</u>
- Parent is a dislocated worker

How Does The College Know If Your Data Is Accurate?

The FAFSA is not a perfect measure for determining a family's financial need. Transposition errors can occur and differences can be bypassed by system edits that can adversely impact the calculations. The good news is that the FAFSA provides the flexibility to make multiple corrections, though there are exceptions that should be communicated directly to the college.

Example: The FAFSA for the 2015-2016 academic year starting in September 2015 will use the 2014 tax return for calculating a family's EFC. The challenge or opportunity associated with this scheduling is that a lot can happen between January 2015 and September 2015 that is not reported on the FAFSA. Since such changes will not be recognized until the 2016-2017 FAFSA, the only recourse is to advise the college about what is going on. Such things as job and family loss, extraordinary expenses, changes in marital status, etc. are some of the many factors that can impact the FAFSA results and should be reported to each college for their consideration.

Once the FAFSA is initially submitted, each filer will receive ongoing reminders from the FAFSA processor that it needs to be corrected with actual tax information. Because of consumer fraud and past abuses, the FAFSA now requires proof and additional steps that validate that an individual's actual tax return agrees with what was filed with the Internal Revenue Service. This is a necessary step that is normally required before any federal funds can be disbursed on the student's behalf.

What If My Taxes Have Not Been Filed?

The benefit of filing a FAFSA as early as possible is to improve the chances of financial aid before it is depleted. That said, doing it much earlier than the IRS April 15th tax-filing deadline creates a much longer gap before the FAFSA is finalized. As a result, the simple, one time FAFSA is not possible. The FAFSA should initially be submitted as close to January 1st, as possible and updated after taxes are filed. Several weeks or months after that it can be linked to the IRS to download an individual's tax filing data using the IRS Data Retrieval Tool system. https://fafsa.ed.gov/help/irshlp9.htm.

Can The College Change The Data On The FAFSA?

If colleges discover conflicting and/or erroneous information from other verifiable documents, errors and omissions, they can correct the FAFSA data. These errors can be minimized with professional help that can identify potential red flags and understand where colleges are focusing and which back-up information may be needed.

How Does The Information Get To The College?

1. Students (parents) complete the application that is transmitted on-line to the FAFSA Processor, an organization that serves as the data entry processor under contract with the US Department of Education. It can also be completed on paper, but keep in mind that it is a much slower process.

2. The CPS, Central Processing System operates under contract with the US Department of Education to receive and process application and correction information. It receives Web submissions, edits and matched data, calculates EFC, and generates all of the processing results.

3. It matches records with the Social Security Administration, Department of Homeland Security, and the IRS in conjunction with the IRS Data Retrieval Tool.

4. The CPS prints and mails the information to students electronically or mails it via a report called the SAR (Student Aid Report).

5. It makes processed data available to each college through an ISIR (Institutional Student Information Record) transmitted to schools, servicers and state agencies.

6. The process is repeated with each submission and update.

What Other Documents May Be Needed?

If an individual's required income tax return data is unavailable, a college may require him/her to obtain an IRS Tax Transcript (http://www.irs.gov/Individuals/Get-Transcript) that provides all of an individual's tax return information. This may be necessary when considering the fact that it takes at least a couple of weeks before the IRS Data Retrieval Tool is available to download your data. It could also take up to several months if taxes were owed on tax returns filed manually.

Some colleges may even request actual tax returns and W-2s for a process called *Verification*. These returns can either be sent directly to the college or via a document imaging service called IDOC (https://idoc.collegeboard.org/idoc/index.jsp.)

What Qualifies A Student As Being Independent?

One of the more common questions that I hear from parents is: What will it take to increase our financial aid by qualifying the student as independent? The advantage of filing as an independent student is that only the student's and not the parental income or assets are reported. This ultimately results in a much lower EFC.

The criteria for determining dependency status are defined on the FAFSA by answering. "Yes" to one of the following questions in addition to providing supporting information:

- Working on master's degree program.
- Active duty in the US Armed services for purposes other than training.
- Have children for which you are providing more than half of their support.
- Have dependents with whom you are living and are providing more than half of their support.
- Both parents are deceased, in foster care, or a dependent or ward of the court when age 13 or older.

- Emancipated minor as determined by a court in the individual's state of legal residence.

- Homeless unaccompanied youth determined by the school district, or high school, or the U.S. Department of Housing and Urban Development.

What Qualifies A Student To Receive In-State Tuition At A Public Out of State College?

Residency Rules:

Out of state residents attending public state colleges pay a premium for tuition and fees. The good news is that some state colleges provide financial breaks for those living in border communities and within certain geographic distances from the colleges. Other states like those in New England have a program (Tuition Break) that offers a discounted, out-of-state tuition rate if a certain major is not offered in a student's state of residency.

The general rule is that state residency requires that a family (not just the student) live in-state, pay taxes, and establish primary residency in that state for at least a year before the academic year to qualify. Living with relatives that are not custodial parents, having an off campus apartment, and working out-of-state with an out of state driver's license while the student's family permanently resides in another state does not normally fall within the definition of being an in-state resident. For this reason, it is best to check with the state college in question to learn about any discounts that may be available. A recap of each state rules can be found at: http://professionals.collegeboard.com/testing/international/state.

How does the CSS / Financial Aid Profile Differ from the FAFSA?

The CSS/ Financial Aid Profile ® (http://student.college board.org/css-financial-aid-profile), which is similar in purpose to the FAFSA in determining EFC for institutionally based financial aid, is a much more comprehensive form. Another version of this form is also available for international students. Unlike the FAFSA, changes can only be made by the college rather than on-line.

Here is a list of some of the additional information reported on the CSS/Financial Aid Profile:

- Current, previous and projected earnings to capture income history.
- Expenses related to education, medical, and mortgage expenses.
- Business value and debt.[9]
- Names, grade level, school names, and tuition for each child in the household.
- Home equity and monthly mortgage amount.
- Tax return detail by line number.
- Retirement Savings.
- Educational debt.
- Current employers, job titles, and years employed.
- Non-custodial parent demographics and contact information.
- Supplementary questions requested by certain schools which can include such things as auto ownership, religion, place of worship life insurance values, foreign investments, and so on.

The /Non-Custodial Profile (https://ncprofile. collegeboard.com)

The need to complete this form is determined by the answers from the CSS/Financial Aid Profile. Although this form is less extensive than the CSS/Financial Aid Profile, it addresses questions relating to child support or alimony paid to the custodial parent as well as the amounts received if the non-custodial parent remarries and is receiving child support from another relationship. This information is prepared separately and confidentially by only the non-custodial

---

9 Note: Some colleges may also require a Business /Farm Supplement form to verify how net income and asset value were derived.

parent but needs to be consistent with the some of the related information reported with on the CSS/Financial Aid Profile.

College Forms will vary but are generally much more straight-forward. The college financial aid office will usually send notifications of additional forms and information.

CHAPTER 10

Should You Plan To Receive a Scholarship?

"If you don't toot your own horn, don't complain that there's no music."

- Guy Kawasaki, *Enchantment: The Art of Changing Hearts, Minds, and Actions*

Scholarship searches, networking, and perseverance are necessary strategies to identify and reap merit-based scholarship aid. Finding scholarship money is not an arbitrary process of submitting as many applications as possible and hoping for the best. If that were the case, chances of receiving anything substantial are slim to none. This happens frequently, especially when there is a lack of focus or control over a process in which others are actively competing for limited financial resources.

Students are fortunate to have the Internet and social media in addition to reference books, suggestions from guidance counselors, friends, families, affiliations, organizations and so on. However, none of these resources offer free delivery or suggest that there is no competition. They are all looking for best candidates that deserve what they have to offer. Therefore, it's the student's mission to discover the amount of the award (scholarship), and doing what it will take to be recognized and deemed worthy of further consideration.

With such a goal in mind, the simple words CAN DO describe the important steps that students should take towards finding scholarship opportunities:

C stands for concentration. It is important to restrict the search and contacts to areas that will reward achievements and qualifications. Beyond the colleges to which the student is applying, scholarships can be discovered on the Internet, on social media, through networking, or by reading as much as possible on the subject.

A is for action. Scholarships don't just happen. Students should take action before their senior year when there is time to strategize and be more resourceful, and enable them to succeed.

N is for networking. This is one of my favorite topics, as it has taken me years to develop the confidence to build a strong network of contacts that have helped me to land jobs and accomplish many goals. Effective networkers need to take the time to formulate questions and get to the right people rather than sending out random e-mails, text messages, or calling someone that is too busy to talk. This is called "target marketing," and in this case, students are marketing themselves while exploring scholarship opportunities.

D is for decision making and adhering to dates and deadlines. Scholarship applications are date sensitive. Students should keep a calendar of critical filing dates but submit them well in advance of the deadline.

O is for being organized and focused. Students should do a little bit each day, even by going after smaller state and local scholarships. It is important to realize that small scholarships with less competition can add up.

1. General Guidelines to Consider

- Always have another person review the student's scholarship essay for accuracy.

- The essay should be original but focused on answering the questions.

- The student should tell a unique story or compelling way to express the need for the scholarship.

- Essays should not be too flowery or brag about accomplishments.

- Focus on the rules and do not submit more than what is required.

- Students should begin the scholarship application process during their junior year to ensure that they know what the provider of the scholarship is looking for.

- If the scholarship requires students to take part in a live interview, they will want to rehearse their answers and solicit constructive feedback.

- Students should check the number of awards that are offered to decide whether they have a chance of getting one.

- A student should never be afraid to ask for a local scholarship, but should be polite if the answer is "NO".

- Students should ask the college that they hope to attend how outside scholarships will impact their financial aid awards.

- As always, students should stay well organized and in control of the process.

2. Functional Resume

The best way to land a scholarship is not necessarily from a website, book, or by paying someone to find one. It takes a combination of factors that bear many similarities to those seeking jobs in a competitive job market.

Start the process by having the student develop a functional resume to summarize accomplishments to build confidence for completing scholarship applications. This resume should include:

- All of the typical, major categories including Leadership, Academics, Awards, Community Service, Extracurricular activities and so on.

- Personal accomplishments to make a student stand out from the crowd.
- Personal milestones in which initiative was taken and positive results were attained.
- Students should focus only on their years in high school.
- They should also share the results for feedback from friends, family and teachers.

Example student resume:

Samuel Reid
3 Wickett Street
Canton, MA 02021

Collegiate Objective: Learn to make a positive contribution to our society.

Leadership
- Class President (12)
- Captain-Debating Team (11,12)
- Vice President-Student Counsel (10,11)
- Created: Hunger for Knowledge Program
- President: Junior Achievement

Academics
- Achieved 3.9 GPA
- National Honor Society (11,12)
- All Honors Program (10,11,12)
- Student of the Year (11)
- National merit scholar

Community Service
- Cradles to Crayons Co-Coordinator
- Canton Food Pantry
- Habitat for the Humanity Leader
- Walk for Hunger Organizer
- Special Olympics mentor

Extracurricular Activities
- Key Club (10,11,12)
- Spanish Club (10,11,12)
- School band (Clarinet) (9,10.11.12)
- Chess club (10,11)
- Girls soccer team (9,10,11)

3. Simple Strategies

- Conduct Internet searches using keywords like "Scholarships for biology majors."

- Write compelling letters to businesses and organizations.

- Contact professional organizations to seek scholarship opportunities.

- Check with Chambers of Commerce's for local scholarships.

- Network with college students to learn their scholarship secrets.

- Check with guidance departments for local scholarships.

- Ask about college scholarships during your campus visit.

- Communicate with writers of stories that may generate scholarship leads.

Categories

Students should also look into any private scholarships. Their searches should include:

- Any specific fields of study that interests the student or applies to their college major.

- Civic organizations that they are currently or have been involved with in the past.

- Labor unions that they are either a part of, or their parents are a member of.

- Religious and ethnic groups that also offer scholarships for active members of their communities.

- Occupations that are related to the student's college major.

- Any and all academic, athletic, and artistic talents that apply to the student.

- Community service and/or leadership scholarships that relate to their high school experiences.

- Horatio Alger stories in which they hit bottom only to rise to the top.
- Professional organizations in which the student is interested in or has experience with.

Scholarship Specific Websites

Below are some scholarships websites to get students started on their search:

- http://www.zinch.com is a one-stop-shop for scholarships.
- https://www.scholarships.com allows you to pinpoint specific scholarships by your major, year in school, and location,
- http://www.studentscholarships.org features career profiles for many fields of study, giving its users an idea of expected salary and job opportunities after graduation.
- https://www.scholarshipexperts.com is a fast and easy resource for scouring the Internet for great monetary awards during your undergrad years.
- http://www.supercollege.com/scholarships/scholarships.cfm is an on-line database of scholarships, grants, and fun contests for undergrads to enter and (hopefully) win.
- http://www.stateuniversity.com/financial-aid/
- http://www.scholarship-page.com/scholarships/

4. Scholarship Control

Some basic steps for ensuring that students have a handle on the process of finding and applying for scholarships are as follows:

- Students should determine their odds of winning the scholarship by knowing the number given and the number of participants.
- They should search for scholarships on the local, state, national, collegiate civic and professional levels.

- Both students and family members should conduct searches by reading on-line and printed articles, conducting Internet searches, using social media and networking with friends, family, guidance counselors and anyone willing to provide a good lead.

- They should be selective and focused on the scholarships that are a good personal fit.

- Students should develop a control sheet similar to the one below to manage their scholarship campaign.

Scholarship Name	Deadline Date	$ Amount Awarded	Essay Name	Notification Date

A selection committee usually decides on scholarship winners in much the same manner as selecting job and college applicants. Each is based on qualifications, standards and tiebreakers that can be in the form of essays or interviews. Smaller and less competitive scholarships may even be based on fewer standards or qualifications such as those in the categories already listed. Students should remain positive and apply to those in which they are strong competitors.

How Do Outside Scholarships Impact Financial Aid?

Scholarship policies vary by college. Many colleges may ignore scholarships that are paid directly to the student although it should be counted as a student's assets. Some may use the awards to reduce the amount of unmet need and then offset the grants and loans. It is always best to clarify the schools policy when discussing it with admissions and financial aid representatives.

CHAPTER 11

Are You Prepared To Apply For A Loan?

"Don't go around saying the world owes you a living. The world owes you nothing. It was here first."

- Mark Twain

Finding the right lender and loan is a necessity for families that are in need of financial assistance to pay for college. Borrowing provides a simple solution and a convenient way to cope with college costs for credit worthy families who are confident about making timely repayments. However, the borrowing experience can be just the opposite for those whose payments are delinquent and subject to costly interest and penalties. When this occurs both the student and parental or other co-signers can be subject to lower credit scores that increase future borrowing costs and eligibility, detract from employment opportunities, and lower net pay subject to garnishment withholding.

I share these facts as I have in my article; Establishing Good Credit is As Important as Receiving Your Degree, found in my website-www.financialaidconsulting.com, to emphasize the benefits and risks of borrowing and the importance of becoming an educated consumer. It is also intended to implore students to make wise borrowing decisions and comply with repayment schedules to build a good credit history to improve borrowing options and secure favorable rates of interest after college.

What Are The Most Important Things To Know About Student Loans?

Borrowers should be just as prepared to compare loan costs and features as they were when evaluating colleges. The list of items that should be considered need not be complicated as long as it addresses the major factors that impact costs and conveniences. Here are some factors to consider:

- Fixed or Variable Interest Rate.
- How often rates change.
- Origination fees.
- Co-Borrower risk.
- Co-Borrower release.
- Credit worthiness criteria.
- Late payment interest and fees.
- Grace period before repayment.
- Loan deferment, forbearance opportunities.
- Repayment options.
- Loan forgiveness.
- Refinancing and consolidation options.
- Customer service and support.

What Are Some Consumer Publications To Better Understand Credit?

- Consumers Guide to Credit: http://www.federalreserve.gov/creditcard/
- Consumer Information About Money and Credit: http://www.consumer.ftc.gov/topics/money-credit

- Cosigning a Loan: http://www.consumer.ftc.gov/articles/0215-co-signing-loan
- Truth In Lending Act: http://www.fdic.gov/regulations/laws/rules/6500-200.html#fdic6500101#fdic6500101

What Borrowing Opportunities Are Available?

There are a wide array of loans to pay for college available to parents and students as long as the borrower can make unemotional and rational decisions that are in the best financial interests of the family. Below is a case study that helps clarify what is meant by unemotional and rational decision making:

Case Study:

I had an interesting discussion about consumer behavior with a business manager that worked for an automotive dealership whose job it was to sell options and additional services after an individual negotiated a deal on their vehicle. He explained that buyers exhibit great energy, fear and a fighting spirit to work out the best deals to negotiate a new car purchase. After the deal, they felt a sense of relief and euphoria before letting their guard down. At that point, business managers go for the so-called "kill" to offer very profitable loan deals, extended warranties, and extras. These are not bargains but appeal to those who are more relaxed and in the mood to say, "What the heck, why not?" Often, these customers don't bother to review the loan disclosures or read the fine print. All they care about is their monthly payments and driving their shiny new car.

This same scenario occurs when parents are so excited about college acceptances that they make emotional and/or costly decisions without taking the time to explore their options.

What Are The Kinds Of Loans To Consider?

There exists an incredible assortment of loans to consider to fund a student's college education. It would be difficult to recommend any one over the other considering the many variables that apply to a family's credit worthiness, financial position, and personal values about borrowing and debt accumulation. The following are merely overviews of the many options that should be taken into consideration.

1. Federal Student Loans

Federal student loans may not be the cheapest but provide greater repayment flexibility and forgiveness for financial hardships and loss of lives. Some loans can also be forgiven for public and military service and teaching. More on this subject will be discussed in Chapter 13.

Subsidized Stafford Loans

Students that complete a FAFSA are eligible for a Subsidized Stafford loan if a family demonstrates financial need. The government will then pay the interest while the student is in college. The following tables illustrate eligibility for certain undergraduate, independent and graduate students:

Dependent Undergraduates

Year	Maximum Subsidized Amount	Unsubsidized	Annual Total
First	$3,500	$2,000	$5,500
Second	$4,500	$2,000	$6,500
Third and fourth years	$5,500	$2,000	$7,500
Aggregate Max	$23,000		

Independent Undergraduates Or Parents Not Approved For A Parent PLUS Loan

Year	Maximum Subsidized Amount	Unsubsidized	Annual Total
First	$3,500	$6,000	$9,500
Second	$4,500	$6,000	$10,500
Third year and fourth years	$5,500	$7,000	$12,500
Aggregate Max	$23,000	$34,500	

Graduate And Professional Students

Year	Subsidized	Unsubsidized	Annual Total
First	Not Available	$20,500	$20,500
Second	Not Available	$20,500	$20,500
Third Year and fourth years	Not Available	$20,500	$20,500
Aggregate Max including undergraduate loans		$138,500	

Unsubsidized Stafford Loans

Students that complete a FAFSA are eligible for an unsubsidized Stafford loan without regard to financial need or assets. Interest on an unsubsidized Stafford loan accrues or accumulates starting when the loan is disbursed.

Year	Dependent	PLUS Loan Denials	Independent and PLUS Loan Denials Annual Totals
First	$5,500	$4,000	$9,500
Second	$6,500	$4,000	$10,500
Third Year and fourth years	$7,500	$5,000	$12,500
Aggregate max	$31,000	$57,500	$57,500

Pros

- Gives the student an ownership stake in paying for college
- Flexible repayment options
- Loan forgiveness and forbearance programs

Cons

- Limited borrowing does not cover most unmet needs
- Interest rates are not fixed and change annually
- Still require origination fees

Perkins Loans:

Students that complete a FAFSA and demonstrate financial need are eligible for this subsidized student loan. The student <u>pays only 5% interest</u> on the loan balance beginning nine months after graduation. The government provides colleges with limited Perkins loan funding that they distribute accordingly.

Perkins Loan Limits

Year	Undergraduates	Graduates / Professionals
Maximum Annual Amounts	Graduates / Professionals	$8,000
First	$5,500	$8,000
Second	$5,500	$8,000
Third year and fourth years	$5,500	$8,000
Undergraduate		
Aggregate Max	$27,500	$60,000*
Aggregate Total	$27,500	$60,000

*Includes maximum amounts borrowed as an undergraduate

Pros
- Gives the student an ownership stake in paying for college
- Flexible repayment options
- Loan forgiveness and forbearance programs

Cons
- Borrowing does not cover most unmet needs
- Interest rates are fixed at 5%
- Limited availability by school

Repayment Options For Federal Loans
- **Extended Repayment Plan** offers a fixed or graduated monthly payments for up to 25 years. This plan applies to Direct Subsidized and Unsubsidized Loans, Subsidized and Unsubsidized Federal Stafford and all PLUS loans.

- **Income Based Repayment Plans (IBR)** caps monthly payments at 15% of discretionary income that is readjusted each year based on your family size and income for up to 25 years. (*Discretionary income* is what remains from gross income after the essentials (taxes, food, clothing, shelter, etc.) have been paid.) This plan applies to Direct Subsidized and Unsubsidized Loans, Subsidized and Unsubsidized Federal Stafford Loans, all PLUS loans to students and Consolidation Loans (Direct or FFEL) that do not include Direct or FFEL PLUS loans made to parents and all PLUS loans made to students.

- **Pay As You Earn Repayment Plan** caps monthly payments at 10% of **discretionary income** and is readjusted each year as your income changes. This plan applies to Direct Subsidized and Unsubsidized Loans, Direct PLUS loans made to students and Direct Consolidation Loans that do not include Direct or FFEL PLUS loans made to parents.

- **Income Contingent Repayment Plan (ICR)** bases monthly payments on **Adjusted Gross Income**, family size and loan amounts. Payments change as income changes. This plan applies to Direct Subsidized and Unsubsidized Loans, Subsidized and Unsubsidized Federal Stafford Loans, all PLUS loans to students and Consolidation Loans (Direct or FFEL) that do not include Direct or FFEL PLUS loans made to parents and all PLUS loans made to students.

- **Income-Sensitive Repayment Plans** are **based on annual income.** Monthly payments can be between 4% and 25% of monthly gross income yet the payment must be equal to or greater than the accrued interest. This plan applies to Direct Subsidized and Unsubsidized Federal Stafford loans, FFEL PLUS Loans and FFEL Consolidation Loans.

- **Standard Payment Plan** offers fixed monthly payments of at least $50 per month for up to 10 years. This plan applies to Direct Subsidized and Unsubsidized Loans, Subsidized and Unsubsidized Stafford Loans and all PLUS Loans.

- **Graduated Repayment Plan** starts with lower payments that increase every two years for up to ten years. It is offered to borrowers of direct Subsidized and Unsubsidized Loans, Subsidized and Unsubsidized Federal Stafford Loans and all Plus loans.

2. Federal PLUS Loans

This is the only federal educational loan offered to <u>parents</u> of undergraduate students and to graduate students. Unlike the federal student loans, PLUS loans will take into account adverse credit history. Such history may include foreclosure, bankruptcy, or tax leins in the last five years. PLUS loans allow parents to borrow up to their full unmet need and offer flexible repayment options and forgiveness options.

Pros
- Flexible repayment and loan forgiveness
- Flexible repayment options
- Offers additional Student Stafford loans if denied

Cons
- Parent is on the hook if the student fails
- Based on credit history, not scores
- Interest rates at 7.21% with a 4.292 loan fee*
  *Disbursements made between 10/1/14 and 10/1/15

3. Private (Alternative Student Loans)

Financial lending organizations, banks, and state agencies such as Sallie Mae, Wells Fargo, Discover and Pickett and Hatcher Educational Fund and some colleges offer these non-governmental loans. Most require a credit-worthy parent or other co-signor to back the loan if the student does not repay it in a timely manner. These loans do not provide forgiveness or relief options, as federal loans do. Co-signors should be cautious of the risks involved with such loans before committing to them. Students should be advised to make timely payments and find loans that allow parents to be relieved of their liability when timely repayments are made over a two or three-year period.

Some students may seek alternative loans not requiring a co-signor. These loan amounts will invariably be smaller and incur higher interest because of the risk that the lender incurs.

Pros
- Can borrow up to the full unmet need
- Variable rates based on credit worthiness
- Available from multiple sources

Cons
- No forgiveness for death or disability
- High fees
- Co-signer risk is high

4. Home Equity Loans

Home equity loans can provide an economical way to borrow at a lower interest rate against the value of a family's home. Before borrowing, parents should consider when to borrow, and the total amount for all college bound family members. The downside is that borrowers pay interest on the lump sum of the loan even if payments are deferred for over four or more years. Borrowing against your home will impact your net proceeds if it is sold while the student is in college or during the loan's repayment period. Parents should also consider creating a payment contract with the student as a means of establishing financial accountability if they wish to have the student share some of the financial responsibility.

Pros
- Interest will be lower
- Mortgage interest is tax deductible
- Makes sense if done conservatively

Cons

- Paying interest on money that may not be needed
- Loan approvals are much more stringent
- Parent is on the hook for everything

5. Home Equity Lines

Home equity lines can similarly provide an economical way to borrow against a family's home at a much lower interest rate. The advantage of a home equity line over a home equity loan is that the interest is only assessed of the amount disbursed as needed instead of the full amount. The downside is that interest rates change and may be higher. Parents should, again, also consider signing a payment contract with the student as a means of establishing financial accountability if they wish to have the student share some of the financial responsibility.

Pros

- Interest will be lower
- Use the funds as needed
- Can be used with a payment plan

Cons

- Interest rates are variable
- Can limit funds needed for other uses
- Parent is on the hook for everything

6. Mortgage Refinancing

Before refinancing, parents should do their research to obtain the lowest rates, closing costs, origination fees, and loan duration to determine their payback. Mortgage rate fluctuations and the length of time that the family plans to stay in the home are serious considerations.

The website www.bankrate.com provides excellent tools to help parents through this process.

Pros

- It can lower your monthly payments
- Mortgage interest on a primary home is tax deductible
- Rates are generally lower than student borrowing

Cons

- Closing costs can be high
- No student accountability
- Application guidelines are more stringent

7. Retirement Savings

Making an <u>early withdrawal</u> from a 401(k) plan to pay for education will increase taxable income and reduce need-based financial aid for the next academic year. Individuals can, however, <u>borrow</u> from their 401(k) as much as half or up to $50,000 if the plan allows it, so that interest and principal are to be repaid over a five year period The risk, however, is that if the individual should lose his/her job, the loan will become due immediately. Bear in mind that these funds are for a parent's financial future. They should only be used if the college can provide a superior education and promising future over less expensive colleges. Borrowing from retirement is last resort when all other financing is unavailable.

Pros

- Money may be readily available
- A loan is not taxable
- Interest may be low

Cons

- Tapping into retirement funds
- No student liability
- Subject to continuity of employment

8. State Loans

Some states offer loans to both in-state and out of state students attending in-state schools. Check with your state's department of education to check eligibility.

9. College Loans

Some colleges offer specially tailored loans to their students. These loans should be evaluated in terms of their interest, origination fees, and repayment terms in relation to other options. Avoid trading the convenience of getting an in-house loan that may not be the best deal.

10. Lines Of Credit

Some credit card companies and financial institutions offer lines of credit that can be used for educational and other purposes. The greatest advantage of such loans are their convenience. The disadvantage is high interest and teaser rates. These loans offer a suitable bridge in the event that money is needed in the short term and can be quickly repaid. This is sometimes necessary if deadlines are missed or if there is a delay in processing the paperwork for less expensive loans.

11. Installment Plans

Many colleges use their own or third party payment plans to enable parents to spread a fixed annual contribution to cover some or all of college costs over a number of months with no interest. The only costs are a nominal up-front fee of typically less than $100. These plans eliminate the need to borrow and serve as a payment option to fill in the gaps. Tuition Pay (https://tuitionpay.salliemae.com/TuitionPay/Enroll/SelectPlan.aspx), Tuition Management Systems (https://www.afford.com), and others provided by colleges offer these services.

CHAPTER 12

Do You Find Your Financial Aid Award "Appealing"?

"We should never negotiate out of fear, but we should never fear to negotiate."

- John F. Kennedy

Financial Aid Administrators are authorized to use professional judgment to adjust a family's financial aid eligibility during the appeals process. In turn, families of college bound students should be encouraged to use this process if they can justify their need for more financial aid.

What is Professional Judgment?

Under section 479A of the Higher Education Act of 1965 as amended authorizes the financial aid administrator to use professional judgment, on a case-by-case basis for students with "special circumstances" that affect a family's ability to pay for college. The spirit of this act is to ensure that there is a fair and uniform process in which such an evaluation occurs.

What Do You Want And Need?

The first step of any appeal and professional judgment determination is to understand each financial aid award before deciding what to do about it.

This an example of how I analyzed a financial aid award for a college costing $55,000 a year from which the student received $25,000 in financial aid. Most of that award was in the form of scholarships and grants, but the bottom line is that the parent still needs to come up with $30,000. Follow these same steps in this example to evaluate your financial aid award before deciding if it should be appealed.

Tuition, Fees, Room and Board	$50,000	Direct Costs to be paid to the college
Books, supplies and other expenses	$5,000	Estimated indirect costs to be paid to third parties
Total Cost Of Attendance (COA)	$55,000	Total annual cost for one year of college
Expected Family Contribution (EFC)	$20,000	Calculated from the FAFSA
Unmet Need (COA minus-EFC)	$35,000	Net amount on which the financial aid was based
How Much of the $35,000 in Unmet Need will be covered by financial aid?	$25,000	This represents 45% of the $55,000 Cost Of Attendance
How much of this $25,000 financial aid award was for scholarships and grants?	$19,500	Free money or gift aid represents 78% of the total $25,000 award. It also represents 35% of the $55,000 Cost Of Attendance.
How much of this $25,000 financial aid award was for student loans?	$5,500	The federal Stafford Loan represents the remaining 22% of the $25,000 award.
How much remains to be paid by the family?	$30,000	This equals the $55,000 Cost Of Attendance less the $25,000 in financial aid. It represents 55% of the cost of attendance.
The $30,000 consists of Expected Family Contribution (EFC)	$20,000	Calculated from the FAFSA
And the remaining unmet need not covered by financial aid	$10,000	This is the $35,000 in unmet need less the $25,000 financial aid.

What Happens If You Are Dissatisfied?

Though this is a fairly decent financial aid award, the $19,500 of gift aid or free money only covers 35% of the $55,000 cost of attendance. That leaves the student and parents with 65% of the remaining financial burden. It is at this point that families should decide to fully or partially accept, reject, and whether to prepare to appeal their award. The question becomes: Is it worth appealing and how much is needed to move forward with attending this college?

This depends on whether or not it is worth paying the $30,000 per year in addition to the $5,500 Stafford loan based on the college major and expected value of the degree and college education. Perhaps, in this case, appealing the financial aid award for another $8,000 requesting $2,500 in work-study and another $5,500 in scholarships and grants would increase the $19,500 to $25,000. The added scholarship and another $2,500 in work-study would cover $27,500 or 50% of the $55,000 cost of attendance coupled with the fact that the student will work for some of it. Reducing room and board by commuting, in addition to indirect payments, can also lower expenses.

This college will still require out of pocket costs over $100,000 excluding interest and fees over four years even if more financial aid is awarded. Money will need to be borrowed and may be a challenge for those with poor credit. Parents should consider this fact, especially if there are other children that will attend college within the next few years. In such a case, the family should consider a less expensive four-year or two-year college, transfer program, the military, public service, and so on. These are all good alternatives if the student has a goal and the family can evaluate the out of pocket costs and benefits of their educational options.

What Is Involved With Appealing A Financial Aid Award?

Appealing a financial aid award is a process that requires families to take a hard look at the net cost of college based on the types of financial aid awarded and then determining how much is needed.

Although, it is always worth the effort, families should realize that colleges are not obligated to offer more financial aid especially if there are limited funds earmarked for students with greater needs or that they are recruiting. This is not to say to give up before beginning, but rather to set realistic expectations and have contingencies if all else fails.

Appeal Letters

I have written hundreds of appeal letters. However, I do so with the caveat that the client must have a solid and supporting reason to deserve more financial aid. Before starting, I gather the facts and supporting documentation to review. Then, I ask the questions that financial aid administrators are likely to ask to cover all of the bases. My letters are very respectful, non-demanding, unemotional, and supported by as much data and "back up" as possible. I get to the point right away and strive to state everything on one page. These letters can be sent directly to the college or be used to support an on-campus meeting.

What Are The Other Ways That Professional Judgment Can Be Used?

- **One time taxable income required on the financial aid forms but is not likely to reoccur.** This can happen as a result of severance pay, bonus, inheritances, or other forms of non-recurring income that has already been taxed, consumed, or is otherwise not available for college costs. Such transactions may increase a family's Expected Family Contribution and reduce a financial aid award.

- **Death of a parent** will impact family earnings. Since income during the year of death may have been reported on the FAFSA, financial aid offices may not, but should exclude it.

- **Loss of child support** will reduce untaxed income that is included in total income. Reducing this amount will increase need-based aid.

- **Loss of employment** will reduce earnings although severance and unemployment are still factored into family income. COBRA and other payments due to unemployment should also be taken into consideration.

- **Student's income** can be high before they attend college and later reduced significantly when they are full-time students.

- **Capital gains** can result from one time transactions resulting in sales of inherited or investment properties or redemptions due to emergencies or special needs will inflate and distort Adjusted Gross Incomes that have already been consumed and not available for educational purposes.

- **Parent reports to active military duty.** This impacts family income although it could have a positive benefit in terms of educational benefits for military families.

- **Business income fluctuations** will vary. Parents may have to provide historic records to show the trends over several years along with projections for future years.

- **Retirement rollovers** are normally one-time transactions that may be taxable before they are rolled over into another retirement vehicle.

- **Cost of living adjustments** may occur with job transfers to compensate employees for the expenses associated with cost of living increases that accompany certain geographic areas. This inflates income but does not provide extra dollars to pay for college.

- **Asset values** such as property values can be misstated depending on the methodologies and market. These values can be adjusted based on the evaluation tools recognized by the college.

- **Medical and dental expenses** that are not covered by medical insurance and not reported on the FAFSA can take a large financial toll on the family's resources and disposable income.

- **Exceptional expenses** such as those related to uninsured property, medical care and unforeseen expenses should be well documented and supported with receipts since they are not factored into the FAFSA calculations.

- **Eldercare and special needs expenses** can be incurred when families provide care to sick and ailing parents and special needs children and others for whom they care. Some of these expenses may be incumbent on the student's parents to pay.

- **Parental educational** debt may be incurred for job training or parental student loans when they were in college. These expenses are not factored into the FAFSA formula.

- **Consumer debt** is not factored into the FAFSA formula or taken into consideration when it is used to cover extraordinary and unexpected expenses for which the parent had no other means to cover.

- **Family** size can also impact financial need when caring for parents, relatives, friends, other students, etc. who require additional financial support.

- The **Higher Education Act** also allows a Financial Aid Administrator (FAA) to use Professional Judgment to make a Dependency Override to the FAFSA to change a student's status from dependent to independent based on written statements and supporting documentation. In turn, their dependency status would exclude parental data and make the student needier. However, a dependency override is not allowed when:

  - The parents refuse to contribute to the student's education.

  - The parents are unwilling to provide information on the FAFSA or for verification.

  - The parents do not claim the student as a dependent for income tax purposes.

  - The student demonstrates total self-sufficiency.

Meeting With A Financial Aid Officer

On site meetings and/or correspondence should be polite, purpose driven, and respectful of the other person's time. Start off with a simple thank you and be prepared to answer the question: How can I help you today? *The best answer is: We are here to ask for your consideration and financial support to enable our child to attend college.* Parents should then be prepared to have the appropriate "back up" information to present their case. They should also do the following:

- Be open minded to low-cost loans and work study to show the willingness to assume some financial responsibility.

- Provide a detailed analysis of incomes and expenses to show cash flow and actual need.

- Be prepared to explain the amount of consumer debt and why it was used for an emergency or last resort to pay for necessities.

- Document unforeseen expenses, loss of employment, death, sickness, and other items that have drained the family's resources.

- Avoid phrases like: "It isn't fair" or "You owe it to me."

- Be open-minded to work-study opportunities.

- Don't compare awards to another student's as each situation is unique

- Be realistic but also ready to move on if a financial aid award appeal is denied.

CHAPTER 13

Is There Some Relief In Sight?

"Plop, plop, fizz, fizz, oh what a relief it is. Plink, plink, fizz, fizz."

- Alka-Seltzer TV Commercial.

Beyond the up-front expenses of paying for college are the tax breaks, loan forgiveness professional and military grant programs that provide welcome financial relief. Here is an overview of some of these programs:

1. Federal Tax Relief Programs

IRS Publication 970, Tax Benefits for Education http://www. irs.gov/pub/irs-pdf/p970.pdf provides an in depth explanation and eligibility requirements for all federal tax relief programs for education. Some are based on income limitations and cannot be taken in addition to or combined with other tax credits. Check with a tax professional to evaluate your tax status and options.

Federal Tax Credits Overview

American Opportunity Tax Credit	$2,500 tax credit per eligible student
Lifetime Learning Credit	$2,000 credit per tax return
Student Loan Interest deduction	$2,500 reduction in income subject to federal income taxes
Tuition and Fees Deduction	$4,000 reduction in income subject to federal income taxes

Source: IRS Publication 970: Tax Benefits for Education pages 86 and 87

American Opportunity and Lifetime Learning Credits

The **American Opportunity Credit (AOTC)** allows up to a $2,500 annual tax credit per eligible student for course related tuition, enrollment fees and course materials for the first four years of post-secondary education. The student must be enrolled at least half-time for one academic period that begins during the tax year pursuing a program that leads to a degree or other recognized educational credential. The current Modified Adjusted Gross Income Limit for this credit is $180,000 for married couples filing jointly, and $90,000 for single, head of household, or qualified widow or widowers.

Accredited public, nonprofit, and private postsecondary institutions such as colleges, universities, vocational schools, or other post-secondary educational institutions are required to provide the student with a form 1098-T Tuition Statement (http://www.irs.gov/pub/irs-pdf/f1098t.pdf) to report the amount received or billed for qualified tuition and related educational expenses. Unfortunately, many families may overlook the education tax credits if they are either unaware of this form or the potential tax benefits for which they may be eligible. Here are some things to consider:

- Parents should advise the student to give them the form 1098-T even though their name is on it.

- The parents can take this credit if they claim the student as a tax exemption even if the student did not contribute to their education.

- A student can claim the tax credit if they take the tax exemption and are not listed as a dependent on their parent's tax return.

- Parents cannot take the credit if their filing status is married filing separately.

- Income limitations do apply.

- Taxpayers can file amended tax returns to recapture these credits per IRS regulations that applied to the years that they could have been taken.

The Lifetime Learning Credit allows up to a <u>$2,000 annual tax credit per tax return</u> for related tuition, enrollment fees, and course materials for one or more courses for an unlimited number of years for post-secondary education. Courses can be to acquire or improve job skills or lead to a degree or other recognized education credential. The current Modified Adjusted Gross Income Limit for this credit is $127,000 for married couples filing jointly and $63,000 for single, head of household, or qualified widow or widowers. Tax filers cannot take the American Opportunity Tax Credit and Lifetime Learning Credit for the same student and tax year.

Student Loan Interest Deduction allows up to a <u>$2,500 reduction in income subject to tax</u> for interest paid on student loans for qualified education expenses for students enrolled at least half-time in a qualified education program. The current Modified Adjusted Gross Income Limit for this deduction is $155,000 for married couples filing jointly and $75,000 for single, head of household, or qualified widow or widowers.

Tuition and Fees Deduction allows up to a <u>$4,000 reduction in income subject to tax</u> for course related tuition and required enrollment fees. The current Modified Adjusted Gross Income Limit for this deduction is $160,000 for married couples filing jointly and $80,000 for single, head of household, or qualified widow or widowers. Tax filers cannot take both the American Opportunity Tax Credit and the Lifetime Learning Credit for the same student and tax year.

2. Federal Grants

Pell Grants

The US Department of Education guarantees college funds for qualified students if their Expected Family Contribution is below $5,273. Grant values range from up to $5,730 for the 2014-2015 academic year. The University of Baltimore provides an excellent Pell Grant Eligibility calculator at: http://www.ubalt.edu/admission/financial-aid/resources/pell-grant-calculator.cfm? to determine your eligibility.

FSEOG Grants (Federal Student Educational Opportunity Grant)

Participating colleges receive a certain amount of federal grant money each year. Money is awarded to eligible students with "exceptional" financial need on a first come, first served basis. Grants range from $100 to $4,000. Students should check their financial aid office regarding participation and eligibility.

3. Relief for Teachers

TEACH Grants

Provides grants of up to $4,000 per year to students competing or planning to complete course work needed to begin a teaching career. Applicants must sign a TEACH Grant Agreement to serve in a high-need field at an elementary or secondary school or educational service agency serving students from low-income families for at least four academic years within eight years of receiving the degree for which the grant was awarded.

Students must be enrolled in a TEACH Grant-eligible program, meet certain academic achievement requirements, receive TEACH Grant counseling, and sign a TEACH Grant Agreement to serve.

https://teach-ats.ed.gov/ats/index.action

Teacher Loan Forgiveness Program (Stafford and Perkins Loans)

https://studentaid.ed.gov/repay-loans/forgiveness-cancellation/charts/teacher

https://studentaid.ed.gov/repay-loans/forgiveness-cancellation/charts/teacher#teacher-cancellation

This program encourages individuals to pursue and continue working within the teaching profession. It requires teachers to teach full-time for five complete and consecutive academic years in certain elementary and secondary schools and educational service agencies that serve low-income families and meet other qualifications to be eligible for forgiveness of up to a combined total of $17,500 on their direct subsidized and unsubsidized federal student loans.

4. Military Programs

Iraq and Afghanistan Service Grant

https://studentaid.ed.gov/types/grants-scholarships/iraq-afghanistan-service)

Offered to students whose parent or guardian was a member of the U.S. armed forces and died as the result of performing military service in Iraq or Afghanistan after the events of 9/11. They must be ineligible for a federal Pell Grant, less than age 24, and enrolled in college at least part-time at the time of their parent's or guardian's death. The maximum award is $5,730.

National Guard College Plans (www.virtualarmory.com) provides test prep and educational benefits for high school students who are about to apply to colleges in their home state. This is in consideration of their training and possibly active duty services.

Reserve Officers Training Corps (ROTC) is offered by the four military service branches to take a full college course load, military science drills and training by agreeing to full time service. **http://www.military.com/rotc.**

The New GI Bill:

http://www.benefits.va.gov/gibill/post911_gibill.asp

For the first time in history, service members enrolled in the Post-9/11 GI Bill program will be able to transfer unused educational benefits to their spouses or children starting Aug. 1, 2009. This option allows Service members to transfer all or some unused benefits to their dependent children or spouses. There is also a calculator, http://newgibill.org/calculator/, to focus on eligibility based on service and participating institutions.

5. Public Service Programs

https://studentaid.ed.gov/repay-loans/forgiveness-cancellation/charts/public-service

The Public Service Loan Forgiveness program encourages individuals to enter or continue to work full-time in public service jobs. Qualified individuals must have made 120 qualifying loan repayments over 10 years while employed full time by certain public service employers starting after October 1, 2007 until October 2017 to qualify. Any non-defaulted direct subsidized and unsubsidized Stafford loans, Direct PLUS, Direct Consolidation loans Health Professions, and Nursing loans will qualify.

Those eligible must also be employed full-time in any position by a public service organization, serving full time in AmeriCorps or Peace Corps or private not-for-profit institutions excluding labor unions or partisan political organizations that provide emergency management, public safety, early childhood education, public health, library services, and related fields described on the above website.

Segal AmeriCorps Education Award
http://www.nationalservice.gov/programs/americorps/segal-americorps-education-award/amount-eligibility-and-limitations-education

The is a post-service benefit received by participants who complete a term of national service in an approved AmeriCorps program—AmeriCorps VISTA, AmeriCorps NCCC, or AmeriCorps State and National. The amount of a full-time education award for national positions is $5,645 for 2014. It may be used to pay educational costs at eligible post-secondary educational institutions as well as to repay qualified student loans. The dollar amount of a full-time award is tied to the maximum amount of the U.S. Department of Education's Pell Grant, but can vary from year to year.

6. General Federal Loan Forgiveness Programs
https://studentaid.ed.gov/repay-loans/forgiveness-cancellation/charts#direct-and-ffel-subsidized

The U.S. Department of Education has developed a comprehensive list of forgiveness, cancellation, and discharge options for Direct Loan, FFEL, and Perkins loan programs. These include provisions for certain professions as well as death, permanent total and permanent disability, bankruptcy, as well as closed schools. Check their website for further details.

CHAPTER 14

Are You Better Prepared To Cope With College Costs?

"Worrying is like paying a debt you don't owe."

- Mark Twain

What About Your Comfort and Safety?

What matters most is your comfort, safety, and confidence about becoming better prepared to choose the educational institution that satisfies the student's academic needs within the family's budget. To that end, I hope it was a pleasant and rewarding journey.

A COPING RECAP

I'd like to share my final acronym for COPING to recap this theme:

Communications is the first step to ensure that families are on the same page about college costs, career planning, campus tours and courses of action to take for evaluating options. Consideration should also be given for using qualified and reputable financial aid and other qualified consultants that can provide value added services to keep both parents and students focused on making the right decisions.

Organization is critical for managing the paper and on-line data that will come to parents and students. Maintaining this information is a partnership in which both the parent and student should share responsibility for simplifying data flow for better internal control. Create simple spreadsheets to condense this data whenever possible.

Planning: It is never too early to plan ahead as long as there is a goal in mind. It involves campus tours, adhering to deadlines, understanding financial need, and finding credible information sources to minimize rework.

Information Gathering: Managing almost unlimited information sources can be overwhelming. Decide which information is needed and the best sources that provide it.

Networking develops strong relationships and insightful advice. It is an opportunity to learn about success and failures from others and get a jump-start on an often-overwhelming journey. It also requires respect of other people's time and a knowledge of what questions are most prudent to ask.

Goal Setting can be as simple as wanting to go to college but must be more specific in terms of defining career interests and projected earnings in relation to the most affordable institutions that can prepare the student for a more promising future. Set realistic goals rather than leaving it all to chance for which you have no control.

> *Obstacles are those frightful things you see when you take your eyes off your goal.*
>
> *-Henry Ford*

I welcome your feedback and the opportunity to provide outstanding professional support. Please visit my website at www.financialaidconsulting.com, contact me at finaidman@comcast.net, or call 1-866-528-7555 for further information or to arrange a consultation.

Published Articles By Howard Freedman

http://www.financialaidconsulting.com/ MyPublishedArticles.aspx

The following is a list of my many articles that provide further information about a vast array of topics to enhance your understanding of *Making College Happen: The Realities of Coping With College Costs:*

College Search
- Campus Visits For The Home Schooled
- Taking Charge Of The Decision Making Process
- Networking To College
- Summer Could Be The Best Time To Visit And Prepare For College

Editorial Commentary
- Reducing College Costs Starts From Within

Employment
- Age vs. Experience In The Workplace
- You Cannot Learn Too Much
- Becoming A Winner Beyond College

Financial Aid

- College Is Affordable If You Are Willing To Go For It
- Mistakes Parents Can Make When Applying For Financial Aid
- You Don't Need Cash To Pay For College
- Overcoming The Hurdles Of Financial Aid
- Conquering The Roadblocks To Financial Aid
- Overcoming The Fear Of Paying For College
- Overcoming The Barriers Of An Affordable Education
- Understanding Your Student Loan Options

Financial Aid Officers

- Worthwhile Ways To Work With Financial Aid Officers
- Working Effectively With Financial Aid Officers

Guidance Counselors

- Ideas To Help Guidance Counselors
- Financial Aid Is There—Help Students Find It
- Taking Charge Of The Decision Making Process

Majors

- Best Careers For Your Future
- Best Ways To Choose A Major

Money Management

- Ten Cures For Managing Your Money
- Establishing Good Credit For The Home Schooled
- Establishing Good Credit Is As Important As Receiving Your Degree
- Which Credit Card Is Right For You?

Scholarships

- How High Achievers Merit Can Pay For College
- Plan To Receive A Scholarship

Taxes

- How To Get Money Back For College

Transfers

- Transferring To Affordable Four-Year Colleges
- Why Transfer Students Should Plan A Campus Visit
- Managing The Cost To Transfer
- Creating A Lean And Mean Budget Before Your Transfer
- Transferring To A Four Year Program

Glossary of Important Terms

"The beginning of wisdom is the definition of terms."

- Socrates

Making college possible requires an understanding of the terminology as it relates to the overall process of putting all of the pieces together. These are some of the important terms that are likely to be encountered:

Alternative Loans-
Non-governmental private college loans offered by lenders such as banks, credit unions, state agencies and schools. The student or parent can take these loans but the student must have a parent or other credit worthy co-signer to minimize the financial risk to the lender.

Appeal Process-
Formal procedure in which the student or parent can request additional financial aid based on special or exceptional circumstances. In turn, the financial aid officer or committee can evaluate each appeal to decide to what extent additional financial aid should be awarded.

Award letter-
Official financial offer by the college for the academic year. It includes the cost of attendance, financial aid (scholarships, grants,

loans and work-study) and net cost. The award can be fully or partially accepted or rejected. It can also be appealed.

Campus-Based Programs-
Federal financial aid programs that are administered by the college. These include: Federal Supplemental Educational Opportunity Grants (FSEOGs), Perkins Loans and Federal Work Study programs.

Conflicting Information-
Inconsistent and inaccurate data reported on financial aid forms may warrant further review and audit. This can happen based on tax reporting and asset variances or other data that questions the accuracy of the information reported on the financial aid form(s).

Cost of Attendance-
The total projected annual costs of attending a college for the academic year. It includes all costs paid directly to the school as well as estimated indirect costs such as personal expenses, books and transportation. The Cost of Attendance less a family's Expected Family Contribution determines the unmet need on which financial aid awards are based.

CSS/Financial Aid Profile-
An additional financial aid form used by certain colleges using a different institutional methodology the student or parent can request for awarding financial aid from institutional versus federal funds.

Deferment-
A period in which payments on direct Subsidized Federal Stafford and Perkins loans are postponed and interest does not accrue. Interest on all other unsubsidized federal student loans will accrue during deferment period.

Dependent Student-
The dependency status on the FAFSA that determines if both the student's and parent's information are required to be reported on the FAFSA.

Early Action-
An accelerated college application process in which students typically must complete their college applications in November before the new year to be considered early for admission. This is non-binding and students may apply to other colleges.

Early Decision-
An admissions program that requires the student to submit their college application in November for an admission decision before the new year. Enrollment decisions are binding and limited to only one school to which the student can apply early.

Enrollment Management-
Term used in higher education to describe well-planned strategies and tactics to shape the enrollment of an institution and meet established goals. This involves seeking and rewarding certain students that meet and exceed their admission's criteria.

Entrance Counseling-
On-line mandatory information and counseling session required before the student receives their first federal student loan disbursement. It explains their responsibilities and rights as a student borrower before they sign a Master Promissory Note.

Exit Counseling-
A mandatory on-line information and counseling session required after the student graduates or attends school less than half time that explains their federal loan repayment responsibilities when repayment begins.

Expected Family Contribution (EFC)-
An amount that determines how much a family should (but may not be able) to contribute to the student's education for the upcoming academic year. This number is derived from the FAFSA while another EFC is calculated from the CSS/Financial Aid Profile if required by certain colleges.

FAFSA- (Free Application for Federal Student Aid)-
A required federal financial aid application available each January 1st for calculating a family's Expected Family Contribution for determining financial need. It is also required for those without financial need but eligible for an unsubsidized Stafford loan.

Federal Loans-
Stafford, Perkins and PLUS educational loans that are offered through the U.S. Department of Education.

Federal Work Study (FWS)-
A federally supported campus-based part-time employment opportunity offered in some financial aid awards.

Forbearance-
A period of up to a year when monthly loan payments due to certain types of financial hardships are postponed or lowered yet still accrue interest.

Gift Aid-
Financial aid such a scholarships and grants that do not have to be repaid.

Independent Student-
The dependency status on the FAFSA to determine if only the student's income and assets are reported to increase the student's financial need. An independent student must meet at least one of the following criteria: 24 years old and older, married, a graduate or professional student, a veteran, a member of the armed forces, an orphan, a ward of the court, or someone with legal dependents other than a spouse, an emancipated minor, someone that is homeless or at risk of becoming homeless.

Master Promissory Note (MPN)-
A binding legal document that must be signed when you receive a federal student loan. It lists the repayment terms and conditions under which you agree to repay the loan and explains your rights and responsibilities as a borrower.

Merit Based Aid-
Financial aid based a student's academic or other achievements, skills and qualifications. States, college admissions, institutions or individuals usually offer these awards.

Need Blind-
A policy that does not consider an applicant's financial situation in its admissions decision.

Need Aware-
An admissions policy in which the admitting institution considers an applicant's financial situation when deciding admission.

Professional Judgment-
The authority of a school's financial aid administrator to make adjustments to the data elements on the FAFSA and to override a student's dependency status to address exceptional circumstances. This can occur based on supported and well-documented corrections and/or the appeal process.

SAR (Student Aid Report)-
A paper or electronic document generated from the FAFSA that provides information about eligibility for federal student aid, Expected Family Contribution, informational messages and loan eligibility. It is also used as a worksheet for reviewing and correcting data.

Self Help Aid-
Financial aid that includes Federal Work Study and student loans for which the student is responsible. It is a way of offering the student financial responsibility before any free money also known as gift aid is awarded.

Unmet or Financial Need-
This is the difference between the Cost of Attendance and Expected Family Contribution. It is offset by financial aid offered by the school that is awarding it.

Verification-

Process to confirm that the information provided on the FAFSA is accurate. Verification selection can be random or may be required if FAFSA data was incomplete, estimated or inconsistent. The U.S. Department of Education selects some students for the verification process based on established criteria.

Howard R. Freedman, BS, MBA

Founder, Financial Aid Consulting.

For over a decade, Howard Freedman's expertise and analytical skills have helped families make a college education possible. He does this by using his college funding, business, and customer service expertise to provide creative and objective solutions to pay for college. As a result, he has built a loyal and growing client base for which Financial Aid Consulting attributes its success.

Howard is located in Massachusetts and works with clients in person or via the phone, Internet or teleconferencing throughout the U.S and Canada. He does not require long term and expensive contracts and fairly prices his value added services to achieve high client satisfaction, retention and referrals.

Howard was awarded a citation from the Massachusetts House of Representatives for his outstanding achievements as the AC-CESS program manager providing financial aid and scholarship services to over 2,700 high school seniors in the Boston public schools. He has also received numerous letters of appreciation from headmasters, guidance counselors and clients that recognize the quality, value and benefits of his services. Prior to Financial Aid Consulting, he was awarded many other citations and awards for his professional, business, consulting and public speaking contributions and achievements.

He is a member of the Massachusetts Association of Financial Aid Administrators where he served on the technology and newsletter committees and the Massachusetts School Counselors Association for which he contributes to their newsletter. Howard is also an accomplished writer addressing financial, business and college related topics in national educational and financial publications.

Howard is a graduate of the College Board's Financial Aid Institute and received his BS Degree in Business Management from Northeastern University and an MBA from Suffolk University in Boston.

Howard R. Freedman, President
Financial Aid Consulting
finaidman@comcast.net
866-528-7555
www.financialaidconsulting.com

Made in the USA
Columbia, SC
17 March 2019